WILLOUGHBY

The story of an Empire's greatest shame

By

A.E. CONNORS

© 2017 A. E. CONNORS

WILLOUGHBY. The Story of an Empire's Greatest Shame is a work of fiction. Names, characters, places and incidents are either products of the author's imagination or are used fictitiously. Any resemblance to actual persons, living or dead, events, or locales is entirely coincidental.

Second Printing. This book was previously printed under the title of ANZAC ©2010

ISBN-13: 978-0692844946
ISBN-10:0692844945

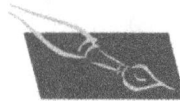

Easytime Publishing

Lake Havasu City, Arizona
www.EasytimePublishing.com

AUTHORS NOTE

Over a period of 350 years, approximately 150,000 British children were deported to Australia, Canada and other parts of the British Empire.

My mother, the inspiration for this book, was one of those children. The daughter of an Australian soldier, she became caught up in the system at aged nine and was later shipped to Canada. My mother, as a child, served in sixteen homes over a period of four years. She made her way back to England at the age of nineteen. Sadly, I could not tell her story. The stigma and shame attached to being a 'Home Child' prevented her from revealing her past. When she learned she was dying she burned every letter, photograph and scrap of paper pertaining to her past life. Only after her death did I learn her real name and circumstances. Since I could not write *her* story I used the research to create, *'WILLOUGHBY. The story of an Empire's greatest shame'* as a work of fiction. My mother died in August of 1995. The records of her life in Canada were received only after her death. The real story she took to her grave.

DEDICATION

This book is dedicated to Mark and to my family. It is also dedicated to the former migrant children who still search for their families back in England and to the Lake Havasu Writer's Group who gave me the support and encouragement to complete this story.

ACKNOWLEDGEMENTS

Front cover photo by Mark A. Connors
Author photo by Ray Kinder

English spelling is used in this story.
Translations: ANZAC.............Australian, New Zealand Army Corp
S'truth............. .Abbreviation for God's truth.
Scrumpy.............A strong cider
Podged..............Bloated stomach. A rabbit malady.

CONTENTS

CHAPTER ONE
WW1

A machine gun chattered abruptly. In the silence that followed, a man's voice called out from the other side of the field in a language most Britons would not have understood. An exhausted English mortar gunner, by the name of Owens, turned to the man beside him. "What's he saying?"

"He wants us to surrender."

Owens voice seemed to rise with each syllable. "Why don't we just go over the top and finish it. We've been pinned down for three bloody days. They're going to kill us anyway!"

John Reynolds, his uniform bearing the insignia of the Australian Territorial Army, was apt to agree. It was a miracle they'd lived this long. John was a tall man with deep-set steel grey eyes and light brown hair. At only twenty-nine years of age he was considered a veteran of the 'Great War'.

To keep themselves above the stinking water in the trench, the two men sat with their backs contoured against one-side … feet braced against the other.

Heavy shelling and constant rain had turned the field, of once red poppies and blue flax, into oozing mud and water filled craters.

During the night dead horses, sprawled bodies and sections of rolled barbed wire appeared as a ghostly scene, in the periodic flashes of white starburst shells.

With the point of his bayonet, Reynolds scraped the mud from inside the barrel of his Enfield rifle. He was thankful the rain had finally stopped. It was daybreak.

The bayonet was reattached and John laid the gun across his lap. He fished around in his breast pocket and pulled out the battered stub of a hand- rolled cigarette. He placed it between his dry cracked lips.

"Give me a light, Owens," he said. His voice was calm and steady. Owens, hands shaking, obliged. Reynolds took a deep drag ... blew on the end and used the hot glowing ember to burn lice from the inside seam of his open topcoat.

"How old are you, eighteen...nineteen?" John asked without looking at the boy.

"Eighteen."

Reynolds pinched off the tip of the cigarette and put it back into his pocket for later. He felt sorry for the young private with the hollow eyes...fighting in a man's war yet not old enough to show even a trace of stubble on his face.

Two nights before, the two had the grizzly task of pulling bodies into the trench to harvest food, water canteens, ammunition, cigarette makings and anything else they could scavenge. They'd have to forage a little further out come nightfall. "How does it feel...to kill someone... close up I mean?" asked Owens.

After the first of the fighting, John thought, he was incapable of feeling anything...his conscience seemed to have calcified for the duration of the war.

Someone once told him that survival was the primary instinct. He'd found that not to be true. He'd gone beyond being afraid of death to a place where there were no emotions. He merely reacted to situations and surroundings without thought of consequence or benefit. How could he explain that to a boy of eighteen?

Before Reynolds could answer, there was a commotion in a grove of dead trees at the edge of the field. Black crows gathered daily to pick at the scraps of human flesh. They scattered as the sound of horses screaming, chains jangling and renewed gunfire filled the acrid sulfur air.

Just as Owens and Reynolds pulled themselves up, to see what was going on, the huge face of a black dog looked down into the trench at them.

"*Jesus!*" Owens exclaimed. Both men dropped into the stinking water below. For the first time the sight of bloated bodies, stench of raw sewage, urine and stagnant water didn't bother them.

Owens lunged at the dog with his bayonet. Reynolds deflected the thrust with his own weapon, grabbed the dog's collar and pulled the animal down into the water.

"Get your shoulder behind those wheels!" shouted an English voice. Both men scrambled to the edge of the trench to see what was going on. Amid shouts and gunfire they saw a team of horses had passed the trees and come to a standstill in the field of mud. "It's a British Artillery Unit!" Owens shouted out.

A mounted Cavalry Officer was shouting encouragement to his men as he pulled on the reins of a lead horse. Covering fire came from the trees. Reynolds could see the terror in the white-rimmed eyes of the horses; nostrils flared as sweat- lathered bodies strained against the weight of bogged down wheels and a heavy gun. Steam rose from the backs of the animals creating a grim tabloid in the early greyness of dawn. Reynolds could see the situation was futile, given the depth of mud and fact that two of the horses were dead in their traces.

Shots rang out from the direction of the German line. The officer and his horse were hit. The horse reared and went down on its side with hooves thrashing as though still trying to run. The officer was thrown onto his back, only yards from the trench where the two men watched helplessly.

"His horse is getting up! It'll leave him out in the open," said Owens. Reynolds shot the horse dead, then reached into the water for one of the dead soldiers.

"Owens, help me get him over the top so I can get underneath," he said.

"It'll be suicide! You won't have a chance!"

"Don't argue with me, boy, pick him up!" Both men struggled to pull the waterlogged corpse up and over the edge of the trench. Reynolds crawled out, under the body, and like a wolf in sheep's clothing inched across the squelching field towards the downed officer.

Reynolds called out to him. "Don't move! I'm coming for you." Owens was having a hard time keeping the dog from going over the top of the trench. It barked and whined.

"Go back!" the officer cried out. "I can't feel my legs… I'll never make it." Reynolds vented a few choice words, took a deep breath and continued his advance.

"When I come over the top of you, grab onto my belt!"

"You can't…I'll be dead weight! You'll get yourself killed, man. Leave me!" Reynolds came over the wounded man. His hands and knees sank deeper in the quagmire of mud as the officer hung onto the belt and said, "You're insane!"

"Save your breath and help push!" Reynolds shifted the burden of the corpse and, crab-like, struggled across the mud with the weight of one man beneath him and the dead soldier on his back. Bullets pinged and thudded into the corpse. The trio made it to the trench but, for a split second, Reynolds left himself vulnerable when he handed the wounded man down to Owens. He knew he was hit but felt no pain.

The Cavalry Officer, his chest heaving as he gasped for air, said, "There are more units coming…we'll have this area secured in no time. You saved my bloody life back there. Thought I was done for. There'll be a medal in this for you!"

There was no response from Reynolds. He was in a world of his own, inside the oblivion of unconsciousness.

Reynolds, as he drifted in and out of the blackness, vaguely recalled lying on one of several canvas stretchers lined up at the side of a road. Shivering, from shock and cold, he turned up his collar and watched the military ambulances come and go. They stopped only long enough to pick up a new load of wounded. He hoped it would soon be his turn.

When Reynolds fully awoke he saw a woman kneeling beside him. She had small hands, chapped from constant submersion in cold water and harsh soap. She wore a man's military jacket over her nurse's uniform. The coat hung open and the sleeves had been rolled up to the elbows. Her skirts were muddy and caked with blood. She had a mass of dark curls that were held in place by a length of string. Her pale and delicate features gave her a look of fragility. She became aware that her patient was awake and looking at her.

"So, you're back with us, are you?" She spoke in a soft English voice and pushed a tendril of hair out of her eyes with the back of her wet hand.

"You're a long way from home," she said, indicating his uniform. Reynolds looked up at the smiling face and sympathetic brown eyes of the pinafored field nurse.

"You were lucky," she said. "There's a bullet fairly close to your hip but, when you get to Paris, they'll take care of it. The head-wound's just a crease…*you'll* live." She smiled at him. Reynolds opened his mouth to say something but the woman stood up and moved down the row to attend the next wounded man.

"Pretty little thing isn't she? Her name's Louise," said a voice from the next stretcher. "I'm James Mannington by the way… Major…Cavalry," he said. "But since you saved my 'arse' back there I suppose you should call me James."

"John Reynolds, Captain, Australian Territorial. What happened to Owens?"

"Sent back to the front with another regiment, I think. We're being sent to a hospital in Paris." Mannington propped himself up on his elbow in order to get a better look at the retreating nurse. Reynolds touched the bandage on his head then winced at the pain the movement caused his hip.

"We're in luck!" said Mannington. "The hospital we're being sent to is a converted chateaux…went to a party there once before the war. The stories I could tell you about that place." Mannington was a confident and articulate man with sandy hair, pencil thin moustache and green eyes. Reynolds observed, even in the dirty uniform, he looked tailored and well put together.

"How badly were you hit?" asked Reynolds.

"Still can't feel my legs…not a good sign is it?" Mannington's smile was brief, his concern transparent.

The massive dog Reynolds had pulled into the trench appeared. Dried mud hung in clumps on its bronze-tipped black coat. With matted haunches it looked like a great bear as it lumbered towards Mannington and licked his face with its huge pink tongue.

"I've never seen a dog that big before," said Reynolds.

"Toby's a Newfoundland." Mannington pulled himself up and ruffled the dog's head. "I brought him with me from home. There are a few of them out here… invaluable to the Army. They've got a natural instinct for rescue work and you should see him in action!"

The pride this man had for his beloved dog was obvious to Reynolds.

"Harnessed to a cart, Toby takes ammunition right to the front lines," Mannington continued. "I should say 'used to' because Toby's going back to England with me, aren't you boy?"

Upon hearing his name the dog intensified its cleanup of Mannington's face.

"Get off me you great stupid dog. You smell like shit!" Toby heard only the tone of affection and continued.

"What do Newfoundland's do, when they're not in the war?" said John.

"Good herding dog."

"Sheep?"

"They'll round up anything… sheep, cattle, ducks, children, enemy soldiers. It's an instinct."

"How do you think that sort of dog would do in Australia?"

"I've never been to Australia."

"Bet he'd be worth his weight in gold there," said Reynolds.

The hospital in Paris was everything Mannington described. Palatial rooms had sheets tacked up around the walls to protect centuries old tapestries. A magnificent multi-tiered crystal chandelier dominated the center of, what was once, the grand ballroom. Lining both sides of the room black iron beds, with stark white linens, looked out of place in a setting of such elegance. Nurses in starched pinafores and caps scurried back and forth across the Italian marble floor. They carried an array of towels, enamel bowls and bandages. John pulled himself up, gritting his teeth against the pain. He looked around for Mannington.

"Right over here!" called the familiar, well-schooled, voice from a bed across the room.

Every man had been bathed and given blue and white striped pajamas. A tea trolley was wheeled down the center of the room and a nurse handed each man, who could hold one, a mug of strong hot tea. Reynolds looked around the room and thought about how clean and civilized it all was… unreal considering the war being fought just a few miles away.

"We're to be sent to a place outside London to convalesce," Mannington announced.

"So I heard," answered Reynolds. "The doctor said I'd be fit to return to duty after Christmas."

"War's over for me."

Reynolds opened his mouth to ask, but Mannington cut him off.

"My legs are paralyzed." He coughed to cover the embarrassment of sounding emotional and felt the need to divert the conversation. "You're an Englishman aren't you, Reynolds? What in the world are you doing with the Anzacs?"

"My father was a sheep farmer from Yorkshire. I had an uncle in Australia who sent money for me to go to boarding school. My father said it was a good opportunity…didn't want me to end up a sheep farmer like him. As for the Anzacs, I immigrated to Willoughby, Australia when I was twenty-two. What about you?"

"I wanted to prove myself. The war was only supposed to last a couple of months. I was afraid I wouldn't have a chance to get into the action before it was over. When I told my father I had a commission, he objected. I'm the last of the Mannington line, you see. What do you do in Australia?"

"Sheep farmer!" said Reynolds and both men laughed at the irony of that.

The convalescent home in London was a far cry from the chateaux in Paris. It was plain and smelled of carbolic soap. Reynolds and Mannington were in adjacent beds in a small ward.

"You've both got a visitor," announced a stout, middle-aged, Matron who popped her head around the doorway.

The slender young woman who entered the room took John Reynolds breath away. She wore a well- tailored grey jacket, black silk embroidery on the bodice and cuffs that matched the ankle- length skirt. Her red hair, swept up in a 'Gibson Girl' style, accentuated the beautiful heart shaped face. Freckles were generously sprinkled, like flecks of gold, across her cheeks and nose and her eyes were as green as…

"John, this is my sister, Phoebe. Phoebe this is…"

"No need to tell me, James," Phoebe interrupted, and walked between the two beds. She took Reynolds hand in both of hers. "You were asleep when I came earlier, Captain Reynolds." Her smile was warm, her voice soft, and Reynolds could smell the wild violet toilet water she wore.

James laughed. "See what you've done, Phoebe, you've rendered him speechless. She always has that effect on men, John."

"Captain, my brother and I would like to invite you to Baden Hall for Christmas, as our guest of honour. Please say you'll come?" John Reynolds hadn't heard a word she said. He was still awe-struck by the beautiful creature standing over him. His silence was taken for acceptance.

"Good! Then it's settled," she said.

During the next month Phoebe visited often. She brought Seville oranges, newspapers and a small bottle of whiskey for her two favourite patients. Her cheerful accounts of books she'd read and 'who was marrying whom when the war was over,' kept both men entertained.

Educated as she was, at twenty- two Phoebe didn't have the maturity to disguise her growing attraction for John.

"She'd be married by now if not for the war," said James. "There's not a man left in England between the ages of fifteen and seventy that isn't wounded. Is there someone special waiting for you back home?"

Before John could answer, the matron bustled into the room and yanked the covers off John's bed. "It's time for your walk, Captain Reynolds."

Each day using a cane for support and sometimes aided by Phoebe, whenever she came to visit, John wrapped his dressing gown around himself and walked the hallway.

He told Phoebe about his sheep station in Australia and of a town called Willoughby. He talked about his parents, who had emigrated with him from Yorkshire, but not once had he spoken of his wife… Maggie.

On one of their promenades down the hallway Phoebe said, "You're improving and in another week you won't need the cane."

"Don't need it now!" said John. "I'm afraid I've been playing the 'old soldier' with you, Phoebe."

"What are you talking about?"

John stopped. With deliberate care he hooked the cane on a hand- rail and demonstrated his recovery. Arms outstretched, he circled then walked back to her with barely a limp.

"John, that's wonderful!" said Phoebe and flung her arms around his neck and kissed him. John was taken by surprise but found himself responding to the softness of her lips and the smell of violets in her hair. He slipped his arms around her waist, pulled her close to him, and kissed her. Phoebe leaned into him.

"Captain Reynolds!" The voice of the matron was like a crack of lightening followed by thunder. "We'll not be having any of that sort of behaviour in my hospital!"

Chin high in the air; Matron strode down the corridor past the two. Phoebe's face was crimson with embarrassment but her eyes sparkled. She smiled and grabbed for the cane but John reached it first and raised it above his head.

"Give me that so I can beat you with it!" she said.

John stuck the cane under his arm as though it were a riding crop. He made his best effort to march in military fashion, as fast as his injury would allow, with Phoebe in hot pursuit.

John stopped with an abruptness that almost caused Phoebe to run into him. He ran his fingers through his hair and turned to face her.

"What is it?" asked Phoebe, her expression full of concern. "You're hurting aren't you? Here, lean on me…I'll help you get back to bed."

"It's not that," said John.

"What then?"

"I shouldn't have done that… kissed you I mean," John said.

"But, why?"

John had just asked himself that same question.

"It's because of the war, isn't it?" said Phoebe. "You don't want to get involved with me because you're afraid you might not come back." Phoebe cupped John's face in her hands and looked up at him. "Listen to me, John. There are no guarantees any of us will be here tomorrow. All that matters is now."

If only it was that simple, thought John. With the women who hung around the camps he had no sense of guilt or conscience. War and loneliness seemed to change all the rules of morality. He loved his wife and missed her. But the truth of it was, after so many years of separation, he could barely recall the details of Maggie's face.

Phoebe was right. He'd be sent back to the front after Christmas and in all probability never make it home. The moment of guilt slipped away as John gathered Phoebe up in his arms and kissed her.

CHAPTER TWO
Baden Hall

On Christmas Eve John arrived at Baden Hall. He'd come up from London, on the late afternoon train, to find a car had been sent to fetch him from the station. He knew a lot about Baden Hall as Phoebe had spoken incessantly about the manor house with its grey stone walls and turret.

"My Grandmother came from Ireland. She used to store cider apples, from the orchard, on the oak floor at the top of the turret. There are stables and a gamekeeper's cottage on the grounds…you'll just love it," she'd told him.

It was everything she'd promised, thought John, as he gazed from the car window at the sweeping carriage-way entrance and winter-bare Horse-Chestnut trees. He was deposited at the front steps, with his valise, where the butler immediately opened the door. John was ushered inside a baronial entrance of dark oak paneled walls decorated with stag head trophies and ancestral paintings. A large round table, in the center of the foyer, displayed a silver tray and an oriental urn of white lilies. The butler looked at the immaculately uniformed Captain with approval. Suddenly, the great Newfoundland bounded out of an adjoining room and almost knocked John down.

James Mannington appeared in a high-backed wheelchair that he expertly maneuvered towards Reynolds. "Toby, that's no way to treat our guest! Hello James. It's good to see you!" John was afraid his look might reveal the pity he felt for his friend, so he waved his hat in a sweeping gesture that indicated the entrance hall.

"This is pretty impressive. What are you…some sort of Lord?" said John.

"Something like that."

The two shook hands.

"Glad you could make it, old man. Come with me, I'll show you the way."

"Didn't know it was 'black- tie'," said John, noticing the attire of his host.

"You look just fine. Thomas will take care of your things and show you to your room. You're late…dinner is in an hour! Good to have you here, John."

A 'gathering of clans' came to mind when John entered the drawing room and was introduced to a large assembly of men and women…friends of the Mannington's. When formalities were dispensed with and glasses filled, everyone turned towards the guest of honour.

"What's all this?" John inquired, feeling uncomfortable about the attention focused upon him.

"A special surprise for the hero," said Phoebe. John turned to look at her. Phoebe's hair was upswept in a cascade of curls. The emerald necklace, sparkling at her throat, matched the off- the- shoulder green satin gown she wore.

Thomas, the butler, stood beside her struggling with a very large wicker basket that he placed at John's feet.

"Open it!" said Phoebe. John stooped down and lifted the lid of the basket. Out tumbled two fat puppies. They were all black except for a white, star-shaped, tuft on the chest. Phoebe picked up one of the pups and turned it to face John.

"They're yours. James is having them shipped to your sheep station in Australia. Apparently you told him they'd be worth their weight in gold."

"I…I don't know what to say." John took the pup from Phoebe and held it up to face him. Its chiseled head looked sculpted and the dark eyes contemplated him with great seriousness. John was obviously delighted but embarrassed by such a generous gift. "They're real beauties. Thank you. I really don't deserve…"

"One of them is Toby's, to remind you of the day you saved my life. The other is from a different line. They'll be on their way to your father, in Willoughby, right after Christmas," said James putting a glass of champagne in John's hand. "Here's to John Reynolds, and all those who can't be with us today," he said. Glasses clinked in the somber silence that followed. "*Hear*! *Hear*!"

Everyone was summoned to the dining room. A long trestle table, covered in lace and linens, stood in the centre of the room. Silver utensils matched the silver edged white china place settings. Crystal candelabra had been placed at each end of the table.

John looked up at the red, white and blue crepe streamers and paper chains that looped from each corner of the ceiling and met at the base of a centre chandelier. He thought about the less elegant Christmas back home. There'd be no ties and tails, evening gowns with sequins and feathers, and no champagne. He wondered if they'd even celebrate Christmas this year.

Phoebe sat opposite John. Her eyes glowed as she looked at him across the candle-lit table. Each guest pulled open a paper Christmas cracker with the person who sat next to them. John flinched at the sound the cracker made. It sounded like the shot of a gun. Favours, prizes, a paper hat and printed riddle spilled out of each cracker.

The Christmas goose was brought in for all to see before it was taken away to be carved and served with roast potatoes and thick gravy. A steamed plum pudding, with rich custard sauce and sprig of holly on top, came next. The conversation turned to how the war was going. John, who had just taken a mouthful of Christmas pudding, coughed and choked. He covered his mouth with his serviette. Thomas stepped forward and gave him a swift thump on the back. John removed a small silver coin from between his lips. Everyone in the room applauded.

"You got the silver three- penny bit. Its good luck!" exclaimed Phoebe. John, his eyes watering from the episode said, "That's wonderful." Everyone laughed. A dark fruit Christmas cake with marzipan and royal icing, decorated with miniature fir trees and a chalk Father Christmas, was served last. The guests retired to the drawing room where carols were sung around an ebony grand piano.

Phoebe stayed at John's side for the rest of the evening. John knew he should tell her about Maggie…but not tonight…maybe not ever. She came to his room, just as he knew she would, and slipped out of the green gown. The passion John felt for Phoebe, amid the scent of wild violets, was real but his heart was still empty for Maggie.

When the Christmas holidays came to an end it was time for Reynolds to leave and head for Dover to catch the ferry back to France. Mannington shook his hand vigorously and wished him well, then Phoebe walked John out to the waiting car. Even in tan jodhpurs, white shirt and brown riding boots Phoebe managed to look feminine, John thought. She kissed his cheek, her eyes shining as she held back the tears for later.

"Take care of yourself, John," she whispered. In the morning fog, as the car disappeared down the driveway, Phoebe waved as she stood on the steps and wondered if she'd ever see John Reynolds again. Fate had it planned that she would.

On a March evening, the wind howled around the corners of Baden Hall while rain lashed against the leaded paned windows. A fire burned brightly in the library causing shadows to flicker on the walls. A mantel clock chimed the hour.

"How long have you known?" asked James, his voice low. Phoebe could see the white of his knuckles as his hands gripped the arms of the wheelchair. The muscle in his jaw tightened as he gazed at the crackling logs in the fireplace.

"It doesn't matter. I wrote and told him. He's an honorable man... he'll marry me."

James exploded with rage and spun the wheelchair around to face his sister.

"Damn it, Phoebe, he was my friend! A guest in my house! How could he do this? How could *you*?"

"It just... happened," said Phoebe. She twisted the silk handkerchief between her fingers. She didn't cry, just looked at the floor. James was reminded of the time Phoebe was seven and had broken the model sailboat his father had given him. "I didn't mean to," she'd said. "Please don't be angry with me, James." This wasn't quite the same as a broken sail-boat.

"Once I'm married..."

"Married? What makes you think I'd allow you to marry him?"

"I don't understand?"

"Look at you... you've never worked a day in your life! Can you picture yourself a farmer's wife? No servants to wait on you? You wouldn't last a bloody week!"

"But I love John."

"Love? Come on, Phoebe, you barely knew him before you slept with him. In the Army we had a name for that sort of woman! "

"But it wasn't like that!" Phoebe shouted back. The stone cold silence, that followed, became too uncomfortable to bear. One of them had to back down and leave the room. Phoebe knew she wasn't strong enough, in the face of the argument. She left the room without saying another word. James's expression was one of triumph.

Three weeks later, Phoebe sat in front of a large oak desk while a florid faced Army clerk shuffled through a sheaf of papers, searching for a particular report.

"Here it is. Nothing new I'm afraid. Like I told you last week, Miss Mannington, Captain Reynolds was posted *'missing in action'*, that's all I can tell you." The clerk looked at the young woman who sat across from him. She was poised and well dressed.

"But you will notify me as soon as you hear something?" said Phoebe.

"Madam… all of us, here at camp, know the circumstances of how Captain Reynolds saved Major Mannington's life. Believe me, we're doing everything we can to trace his whereabouts. The truth of it is that when a *'missing in action'* is filed, nine times out of ten it turns out to be *'killed in action'*. You do understand, Miss?"

"Yes, but I know he's alive. We're to be married, you see." Phoebe sighed and stood up to go. "I'll be back next week."

"Best forget him, Miss," the clerk said. His voice conveyed a tone of sadness.

"Why would you say that?" Phoebe looked alarmed.

"I'm trying to be as delicate as I can Miss Mannington. I don't mean to sound disrespectful but there's no point in you coming here every week. Captain Reynolds, well…he already has a wife."

There was a long silence as Phoebe digested the information. She was unaware of the high colour rising in her face. She could hear her heart pounding in her ears and felt light headed.

"That can't be true," Phoebe whispered. "He'd have said." The clerk pulled a document out of the folder and handed it to her.

The address was Willoughby, Australia.

"There now, you don't look well Miss, can I send for a cup of tea or a glass of water for you?"

Phoebe's legs felt wooden as she walked, in a daze, towards the door.

"No…that won't be necessary, thank you," she said. "I'll be fine."

"I don't think you should leave like this," said the clerk getting to his feet.

"You've been very kind," was all Phoebe said and swept out of the room. She wept all the way back to Baden Hall.

Later, that same day, James Mannington drew his eyebrows together in a grim frown. He refused to make eye contact with his sister.

"I'm sending you to a small convent, in Wales, until the child is born. It'll be put up for adoption. When you return home nobody will be the wiser."

"But James!"

Her brother ignored her. "Afterwards, you'll settle down in a suitable marriage. James suddenly laughed sarcastically. "Can you imagine the tongues wagging? '*Lady Phoebe Mannington... pregnant by a married soldier.*' They'd have had a field day with that!"

"James, I don't want to give up the baby. I…"

"You'll do as I say!"

"What's happened to you, James? I don't know who you are anymore. You're bitter and mean spirited. Life's too short for us to…"

"Too short! Is that what you think, Phoebe? Let me tell you something…every day's a God-damned eternity!" James shouted. "Trapped in this chair is like being buried alive. I'd sooner have died with the lads in my regiment than be forced to live the rest of my life like this!" James hit his fists on his legs and his tone became low and menacing. "The one thing I have… you want to take away from me!" Phoebe stepped back when she saw the look of sheer hatred on his face.

"I have power and respect in this county! My reputation's the only dignity I have left. I won't be made a laughing stock because of you. You'll tell no-one about being pregnant…do you hear me? And don't even think about bringing your little mistake back here… you won't get a foot in the door! A baby born on the wrong side of the blanket tells the whole world you're nothing but a common tart. John Reynolds didn't do either of us any favours!"

"James…please!"

"Leave. I can't stomach the sight of you right now!"

The distorted face that spat out such venom bore no resemblance to the brother Phoebe once knew. James set his chair in motion and headed for the door. Without turning to look at his sister he said, "I'll have Thomas pack your things. You'll leave in the morning."

Phoebe stood in the empty room with her arms folded tightly. Her cheeks flamed with humiliation and her eyes looked towards the ceiling preventing the hot spill of angry tears. James was right. Without his

support she'd never manage. She would have to comply…there was no
other option.

CHAPTER THREE
Phoebe

Phoebe stood on the platform while Thomas returned to the train to retrieve her luggage. The smartly uniformed station master paraded up and down, full of his own importance. He was oblivious to the noise of whistles blowing, doors slamming and hissing steam billowing out from under the massive iron wheels of the train. Each arrival was heralded by an entourage of grey and white pigeons that fussed and flocked at the feet of alighting passengers.

Large wire baskets of red geraniums hung from the eaves of the slated rooftop and the station's clock, large and prominently positioned, commanded attention from everyone. A few soldiers were on the platform saying their goodbyes to tearful family members.

Phoebe noticed the looks she received the moment she stepped off the train. Among the working class people of Wales she felt self-conscious and out of place in her expensive fur trimmed coat and matching hat. A woman with a little girl also felt self-conscious. She was aware of how drab her own clothes must seem compared to this elegant peacock of a woman who flaunted wealth in the face of those who worked so hard and had so little.

Phoebe smiled at the little girl whose mother whisked her away.

"I have your suitcases, Miss. There's a hire-car waiting. Shall we go?" said Thomas.

The convent was an older brick building on the north side of the Sacred Heart Church and school. Phoebe was silent as Thomas placed her two tapestry suitcases in the front hall. A nun, her face pale and ageless, introduced herself as Sister Mary Margaret.

"I'll show you to your room Miss Mannington," she said.

"I'll be going then," said Thomas. He hesitated a moment, reluctant to leave his charge in such a depressing place.

Phoebe was shown to a small room. A single bed was against one wall with a brass crucifix above it. A wood night-table, with a piece of folded paper tucked under one of the legs to stop it wobbling, held a glass oil lamp and a well-worn bible. A four drawer chest sat in front of the window.

"Until your time," said Sister Mary Margaret, "you'll be expected to help in the kitchen. There'll be ironing to do and some cleaning. Light work but it'll make the time go by faster. We all pitch in here."

"But I don't know anything about ironing or…"

"Then you'll learn!" said Sister as she began to unpack Phoebe's clothes. "My word, these clothes won't do! I'll go and find you something more suitable."

Phoebe, left alone, looked at the taffeta dress and linen suit in her suitcase, the silk and lace nightwear and satin slippers. The room was dark and cheerless. More like a cell, thought Phoebe. She sat on the bed with her hands over her face and sobbed.

"Now then," said the nun as she came back into the room carrying a bundle of clothes over her arm, "It's not as bad as all that. Your situation is only temporary, you'll be back home before you know it." Sister Mary Margaret held out the clothes. "You'll find these a bit more serviceable. Get them on and I'll make you a nice cup of tea and show you the garden. It'll cheer you up."

Phoebe held out the coarse brown dress. A beige cardigan sported a darn spot on each elbow.

"I can't wear these! They're awful! Where did they come from?"

"Donations…for the poor. We wash and darn everything before it's distributed. Still a lot of good wear in those clothes. You won't want to wear anything nice for kitchen-work." Phoebe's wails could be heard all over the convent.

On a bleak day, at the end of September, Phoebe's lower back and stomach cramped in wave after wave of pain. For three agonizing days and nights the process of labour brought her to the brink of unconsciousness as she sweated and writhed, in tortuous pain, to expel the child from her body.

Her terror stricken eyes darted around the small room, seeing nothing, as she screamed for the pain to end and someone to help her. The beige cotton shift she wore was soaking wet and her hair was plastered against her head.

"She can't take much more of this, she's starting to go into shock," said Mrs. Williams, the midwife, to Sister Mary Margaret. Phoebe's eyes rolled back until only the whites showed. She rocked her head from side to side and screamed for God to let her die until, well into the third night, at last the baby came.

There was no cry at first. The midwife rubbed the baby vigorously with a rough towel then held the infant up by its ankles and gave the buttocks a good hard smack. The sound was like the crack of a whip followed by seconds of interminable silence. A rush of air entered its lungs and the baby screamed for all the world to hear.

"It's a little boy!" announced the midwife. She held the baby out under his arms.

"Has all his fingers and toes. There's a little purple birthmark on the back of his neck. What we call a port- wine stain, dear, nothing to worry about though."

"Is it shaped like a small leaf?" asked Phoebe.

"Yes, come to think of it, it does look like a leaf." Phoebe smiled. "My father carried the same mark and so do I."

The child curled his back, opened his hands wide and cried in protest of his rough handling. His tiny trembling body was red and wrinkled. Phoebe thought that she had never seen anything so beautiful.

"Oh, listen to you," said Sister Mary Margaret as she wrapped a clean towel around the squealing child and laid him beside his mother.

The elderly nun laughed and said, "He roars like a toothless lion... what we call 'all mouth and no trousers'... and will you look at that red hair!"

Phoebe's smile was angelic when she looked at her baby.

"Welcome to the world," she said to him, and planted a gentle kiss on his forehead. Her voice was hoarse and barely audible.

"Have you a name for him? For the birth certificate," asked Sister Mary Margaret.

"No." said Phoebe.

For a moment, the old nun studied the young woman who cradled the baby's head against her neck. She thought about how much the scene reminded her of the statue of the 'Blessed Virgin and Child,' in the back alcove of the chapel.

Mrs. Williams nodded her head, in the direction of the door, to beckon Sister to follow her to the front hall.

"Just wanted to have a word with you before I left. She needs to go to hospital right away. I'll call on Dr. Llewellyn and send him over," whispered the midwife putting on her hat and coat and then jabbing a lethal looking hatpin through the hat.

"There was some hemorrhaging and I really don't like the look of her colouring. It's her first baby, but it'll be her last I'm afraid. No family then?"

"The man who brought her here, Mr. Thomas, claimed to be an employee of Miss Mannington's brother. He said the baby was to be put up for adoption but Miss Mannington told Mother Superior she was keeping the child… said she'd retained a position as a nanny in London."

"If I were you, Sister, I'd write to that brother of hers. She can't take care of a baby. She'll need months of care and the only place that would take her, without financial support, is no better than an asylum."

Thomas arrived at the convent, a week later, and was ushered into a long sitting room to await an audience with the Mother Superior. The contents of the room consisted of a tavern styled trestle-table, with benches on either side, and a brown overstuffed leather settee with matching chair. A benevolently smiling statue of Our Lady sat on top of an ornately carved medieval sideboard. The only other object in the room was an ivory replica of Jesus who hung from an ebony cross on one of the walls. The sun streamed through latticed, gothic windows making rainbow flecks of light on the foot-worn stone floor.

Thomas was startled when the heavy iron latch of the door lifted and the Mother Superior entered the room. She was a tall and forbidding woman in her black and white habit. Wooden rosary beads hung from her waist. They clicked as she walked and in her wake Thomas detected the faint scent of coal- tar soap. Her face, sheltered from the sun inside the convent walls, was pale and showed a hard constitution. She motioned for Thomas to sit.

"I'm told you wish to see me, Mr. Thomas?" she said, in a tone that conveyed her displeasure at being summoned.

"Yes. Well, I'll get right to the point. I'm here on behalf of Miss Phoebe Mannington. I have a letter," he said, and handed over the cream bonded envelope. Mother Superior put on round wire glasses and tipped her head back a little in order to read.

"It states here that Miss Mannington, having been transferred to a private hospital, wishes me to relinquish her child for adoption." Mother Superior lowered her head so she could peer at Thomas over the glasses.

"Is this true?" she inquired, her voice crisp as winter ice cracking under the heel of a hobnailed boot.

Reciting a well-rehearsed piece Thomas said, "Well, being a titled lady, it's a delicate matter you see. This incident was a youthful digression with a married man. Her brother is counting on your discretion and, I might add, wishes to increase his donation to the convent… to a sizeable amount. Miss Phoebe did sign a release to turn the child over."

Thomas got up from the chair and crossed the room to point out the signature at the bottom of the letter lest Mother Superior had missed it. His celluloid collar suddenly felt too tight and he ran his finger along the inside to loosen it.

"I'll attend to it! The child will be sent to a ministry in London and put up for adoption. I'm afraid this little one will be difficult to place. Not many want a red-headed child."

"And why would that be?' asked Thomas.

"The red hair is a stamp of Ireland in the blood, Mr. Thomas. That predisposes a difficult child with an element of temper. Good-day to you!"

Mother superior was out of the room and gone before Thomas could say another word. He stood there for a moment until Sister Mary Margaret entered the room.

"I'll see you to the door," she said.

"Before I go could I see the boy… just once?"

"I don't think that's…"

"Please!" said Thomas and reached out to touch the old nun's hand. The baby was sent for and handed to him. Thomas bent his head and looked at the tiny infant with its perfect little face and carrot- red hair then turned towards the nun.

"What's his name?"

"She didn't give him one. Felt it best not to, I suppose."

Thomas had lived his whole life at Baden Hall as his father had before him. Like a Chameleon, he blended into every room in the house becoming visible only when required to perform a service. Thomas was trained, from the time he could walk, to be rigid and expressionless. Robbed of his life by tradition, he merely existed. But, something happened when he held the baby in his arms. The child's hand curled around his finger. The tough veneer peeled away leaving his heart exposed.

"Here, you take him, Sister." Thomas handed the baby back. He turned his head away and took a large white handkerchief from his coat pocket and blew his nose. "Thank you. I won't be taking up any more of your time," he said and picked up his hat from the table. He stopped for a moment then turned around.

"Sister?"

"Yes Mr. Thomas?"

"There's something I want you to do for me."

CHAPTER FOUR
Reunions

Early in September, Maggie Reynolds waited quayside at the Melbourne dock. She felt excited but nervous as she watched the soldiers coming down the ramp of the ship. Maggie was a natural beauty with sun-bronzed skin that glowed with a light perspiration in the heat of the day. Strands of copper coloured hair clung to the nape of her slender neck and a breeze ruffled the hem of her pale green frock. She'd worn a pink lipstick, just for today.

Maggie glanced at each soldier's face as she jostled her way through the exuberant crowd… then she saw him.

John was afraid he wouldn't recognize Maggie. He had incomplete pictures of her in his mind. Maybe she'd decided not to come.

"John! Over here," Maggie called out and jumped up and down, waving to get his attention. Her heart beat faster as she made her way towards him. She held back a moment, unsure of herself.

John didn't hesitate. As soon as he spotted Maggie he threw down his kitbag and scooped her up in his arms. He held her so tightly she could hardly breathe. No words were exchanged, there was no need.

After a while John pushed Maggie away from him. Holding her at arm's length he looked her up and down.

"S'truth, Maggie, you're beautiful!" He pulled her close then held her face between his hands and kissed her eyelids, forehead, cheeks and lips.

"I love you John." Maggie's statement was simple but honest.

"I love you more," said John and kissed her again.

The drive home was long. John drove with one hand on the wheel while holding Maggie's hand, tightly, with the other. Frequently he kissed her fingers and turned to look at her. He felt no need for conversation. He just wanted to look at Maggie and listen to her voice.

Maggie was self–conscious about being alone and in such close proximity to John because it felt awkward after the years of separation. She filled the silence with nervous chatter.

"The Army sent all your personal things home…they said you were missing, presumed dead. Everyone in town came to the church service, John."

Even his name felt unfamiliar to Maggie's lips. She felt awkward. Intimacy recalled and anticipated but no way to break through the shell of formality now she was alone with him.

The way John kept looking at her made Maggie's skin tingle. It had been so long since he'd touched her. She envisioned what that would be like when he did and blushed at the thought.

Maggie took a deep breath and prattled on about the weather and the station. "Those two dogs Mr. Mannington, in England, sent were a Godsend I can tell you. The Foreman said each one can do the work of ten men. Your Dad trained them himself. They can cover miles when it comes to moving sheep. Don't seem to like the heat much though, spend hot days in the river."

John pulled the car over to the side of the road, behind a stand of trees, and turned the engine off.

"The whole town's planning a big welcome home party for you this weekend, everyone will…"

"Shut up Maggie," John said and kissed her for a very long time. He reached for the buttons on the front of her dress. Maggie flung her arms around his neck and began to cry.

"I thought I'd never see you again," she said.

When the sheep station came into view, John stopped the car on the dirt road and got out. Maggie joined him. The motor continued to run and the heat made undulating waves above the hot engine. The house, a rambling two-story with upper and lower verandas, was built by John's uncle. It took many full-time station hands and a foreman to run the place. The shearers were seasonal.

Curtains billowed out of open shuttered windows and green pastures stretched for as far as the eye could see. In a tree- shaded corral, stock horses milled about, skittish at the sound of the car engine.

"What is it?" said Maggie as John shaded his eyes against the afternoon sun.

"I just want to stand here and look at the old place, make sure it's real. There's so much space. Back in France...." His voice trailed off as he thought about the confinement of the trenches, the crowded ship. He closed his eyes and filled his lungs with the warm air.

"It doesn't get any better than this, Maggie," he whispered, pulling her close to him.

"Oh, yes it does," said Maggie. "Your Mum's made a mutton roast with mint sauce and those pre-boiled deep fried potatoes you like. Come on, she's waited long enough to see you. She and Dad will wonder why we've stopped short of the house. They'll think we're up to something!"

"Don't give me ideas!" said John and chased Maggie back to the car.

John's mother was a small heavyset woman with a maze of wrinkles on her beaming face and John felt the full force of her as she hurried down the steps to greet him.

"We wanted to come and meet you but I told your Dad it 'ud be best if you and Maggie had that time to yourselves." She held onto John, crying then blowing her nose into a handkerchief and repeating the process. Eventually he had to peel her off him.

"Come on Mum, you're getting me all wet! Where's that dinner? I could smell it all the way from Melbourne!"

John looked over her head and saw his father standing in the doorway. The weather- beaten face was like tanned leather and the old man's bottom lip trembled with the effort to contain his emotions. The two thumped each other hard on the back, as men do, and hugged for a long moment. The old man looked over John's shoulder and into Mum's eyes. When he nodded... she understood. Prayers had been answered...their son had come home.

Over the months, Maggie was awakened each night as recurring nightmares brought John up out of his bed sweating and screaming as he shouted warnings to phantom soldiers in the battlefields of his mind. Maggie never knew there'd been nights, in the trenches, when John was afraid to fall asleep in case he didn't wake up, that other nights he prayed he wouldn't have to.

In the darkness of his subconscious he could hear the shouts of men and the chatter of machine guns. Nightmares of moving pictures replayed as enemy soldiers rose up against him. There was definition in the details of their uniforms but the faces remained featureless and blank. No matter how many times John struck them down, they always returned.

Maggie stroked John's forehead. Held him until he went back to sleep and wondered if he dreamed of Phoebe Mannington and if she, Maggie, would ever tell him that she knew.

The next few years were uneventful as John Reynolds slipped back into the routines of running a large operation. The station flourished, compelling him to take on more help. The demand for mutton and wool increased to the point the whole region became a major supplier. The town grew and its people prospered.

One morning, while making a few minor repairs to the roof, John happened to glance down at Maggie who, with her mouth full of clothespins, was pegging out laundry. Her hair, fighting a losing battle against the wind, was piled high and held in place by a tortoise-shell comb.

As he looked at her, against the backdrop of billowing white sheets, he wondered if she knew how much he loved her.

John's presence hadn't gone unnoticed by Maggie. She removed the clothespins from her mouth and called up to him. "When you've finished with the roof you can give me a hand moving a few bits of furniture. The baby's going to need a room of its own and I'd like to get started on it today." John didn't see the smile that curled the corners of her mouth as Maggie flounced back into the house carrying the empty wicker laundry basket.

"Baby?" John exclaimed as the hammer clattered across the rooftop and fell to the ground. "Maggie, come back here. Did you say baby? You did! I heard you say it. S'truth woman, will you get back here!"

During the next three months the house was alive with activity as the family prepared for the arrival of another generation of Reynolds. John noticed his mother and Maggie talked, secretively, about paint colors, knitted layette patterns and baby names. The family photo album made an appearance and speculation arose as to whom the child might look like. John felt excluded from that closeness only women shared.

The upstairs sewing room was finally cleared and the walls painted a pale lemon yellow. A small white chest of drawers had been filled with cobweb fine lacy jackets, tiny booties and beribboned bonnets. Folded linens and toiletries were neatly stacked on shelves and a galvanized pail sat under a black metal crib. Everything waited, as though the house was holding its breath.

One evening John opened the screen door and came out onto the porch to watch his father smoke an old Brier pipe as he rubbed wax into the hand- carved wood of the cradle he'd made for his first grandchild.

"It's done," Dad said in satisfaction. "Should last a few generations. I'm right proud of how it turned out." He stepped back to admire his work and John could see the pride glowing in his father's eyes.

"You did a champion job on it, Dad. Can we sit for a bit?" Both men stretched out in the sun bleached wooden rockers.

"Only four more weeks 'til the baby comes," said John and drummed his fingers on the arms of the chair. "I'll be glad when it's over, I can tell you. One minute Maggie's crying and the next she's mad as all get out. I just don't understand women."

The old man clenched his pipe between his teeth and laughed.

"None of us do! I know what you mean though. Broody women and all their goings on is hard on men-folk. Your Mum gets twitipated every time the bloody cat has kittens! Doesn't take much to set 'em off either. Have you and Maggie decided on a name yet? "

"It changes from day to day." John grinned. "Maggie wanted Alphonse for a boy and Aphrodite if it's a girl. That was the week of the 'A's but, I think you'll be happy to know, we've finally settled on William or Alice."

"Hope for a boy, lad. I couldn't bear to think of someone else reaping the benefit of all the hard work we've put into this place," said the old man as he gazed out at the star studded night.

The precious moment, shared between father and son, was broken by Maggie who came outside with two mugs of tea. Still a slender woman, but now with an enormous stomach, she shifted her weight from left to right and leaned slightly backward to distribute the discomfort of the growing child. Both men suppressed laughter as she waddled, duck-like, towards them.

"What?" she asked defensively when she saw the amused look on their faces.

"Nothing," said both men in unison.

No-one knew where he came from. He just appeared the next morning standing, like a crane on one leg, under the shade of a Eucalyptus tree about fifty feet from the house. He leaned on a hand-carved staff that was detailed with tribal carvings. A tall, gaunt-looking man with thick coarse hair that stood up… matted, nappy and grey-white. His feet, wide and splayed out, had never felt the imprisonment of a pair of shoes. The soles of his feet were pale, like the palms of his hands, in stark contrast to his opaque ebony skin. His face, with its large pores and wide forehead, showed no emotion. Curious to see whom their visitor was, Dad and John came out on the porch followed by Maggie and Mum.

"Where do you think he came from?" said Maggie. She noticed the canvas bag the man wore, like a sling, over his left shoulder and under the right arm.

"Had to have come down river during the night. The tribesmen sometimes go on walkabouts. Some sort of spiritual thing…don't know much about it myself," said John.

"Could have come from the mission. Clothes don't look too tribal to me," said Mum who noted the man's open cotton shirt and khaki shorts. John waved the man over. Straight –backed he walked slowly using his staff but without evidence of disability.

"Looks more African than Aborigines to me," said Dad. "Could have jumped ship. Most whites wouldn't see much difference between African and Aborigines."

"Are you looking for work?" John called out.

The man smiled, showing missing teeth. "Yes, I am looking for work," he said.

His English was precise.

"You can see the foreman… over there." John pointed to a shed.

"Better come in the kitchen and I'll get you something to eat," said Mum.

"No, Missus. Thank you." He walked off in the direction of the shed.

"Proud…won't eat unless he works for it," said Dad.

Along with the other hands, the new man worked from sun-up to sundown. He cleaned out sheds, repaired fences and dug holes for posts. He ate away from the others and slept under a tree, preferring the outdoors to the bunkhouse.

"How long do you think he'll stay?" John asked the foreman.

"Dunno. Says he's some sort of medicine man. Keeps saying he's *'supposed to be here'*, whatever that means. He'll just up and leave when he's a mind to, I s'ppose. Nice enough bloke, hard worker."

"Did you find out his name?"

"Yes. Bloody long name it was too, couldn't pronounce it. The men decided to call him Henry…seems he likes the name."

Henry's broad feet padded across the wood floor of the kitchen as he brought in supplies and did all the heavy lifting. When Maggie was there he looked at her with great sadness in his eyes.

"What is it?" she'd ask. He watched her when she wasn't looking, still with the same deep sadness.

CHAPTER FIVE
Willoughby

Next morning John and Maggie lay side by side in bed as the aroma of bacon wafted in through the open window.

"Eggs, bacon, tomatoes and fried bread. We *have* to get up!" John said and kissed Maggie on the forehead. "She doesn't make English breakfast that often," he said, referring to Mum. He climbed out of the bed.

"Come back to bed and cuddle for a minute," said Maggie pulling the sheet higher and snuggling into the pillow. John lay back down beside Maggie and pushed her hair away from her face. She moved her head to his chest and closed her eyes.

"I wish you'd wait until Tuesday and let *me* drive you to town," said John.

"Don't be silly. Your Dad said he'd take me. It's just a checkup. I'll be back tomorrow. Besides, you have the tally sheets to do and it's probably the last chance I'll have to shop before the baby comes." Maggie stretched. "I'm going to have a nice wash and get all dressed up, '*like a dog's dinner*'," Maggie said, her eyes still closed, "show Willoughby what I look like eight months pregnant!"

"Do you think they're ready for that?" said John.

Maggie opened her eyes wide, feigned outrage and turned over. She sat up and struggled to get out of the bed but the softness of the mattress, and the awkwardness of her disproportionate shape, caused her to keep gravitating back to the centre. John looked at his wife, in amusement. "You look like a little podged rabbit," he said.

Maggie glared at John and he raised his hands, palms outward, warding off imaginary blows.

"I was just joking!"

"Not funny!"

John pulled Maggie into his arms and they both rolled to the middle of the bed, in a fit of laughter, and then fell silent as they gazed at the ceiling while contemplating the change a child would bring to their lives.

"I love you so much, John," Maggie whispered, turning her head on the pillow to look at him. He saw her eyes were full of tears. "Hey, what's this all about?" said John. He looked concerned as he caressed her cheek.

"I just want you to know how happy I am, about the baby."

"I'm happy about the baby too and..." he kissed her passionately and whispered, "I love you so much, Maggie."

Maggie was excited, a few hours later, when dressed in her new frock she was ready for town.

"Look at *you*!" exclaimed John and wolf-whistled. Maggie turned to give the whole family a good look at the outfit, a blue print two-piece with a white crocheted collar.

"I do love that woman," said John.

"She's a good girl," said Mum. "There's none better than our Maggie. Like my own daughter she is." John grinned. "I told her she looks a bit like a podged rabbit this morning."

Mum gave him a side-long look, jabbed him in the ribs with her elbow, and went back into the house. The car chugged and spluttered then picked up speed as the old man coaxed and cajoled it to life. Maggie waved, vigorously, from the open window while John stood and watched until the car was out of sight. As the dust lingered, against the backdrop of the pale Australian sky, John experienced the same sense of loneliness he'd felt at the dock in Melbourne before he left for France. There would always be a hollow space inside him whenever he and Maggie were apart.

As the town of Willoughby came into view Maggie fished about in the bottom of her handbag for a compact. A few wayward strands of hair were spit curled back under a white sunbonnet. The hat was then tilted at different angles until she was satisfied with the look.

"You women!" Dad said and grinned.

"It's not every day I go to town, Dad. I've been looking forward to it all week."

"I daresay it does get lonely back at the station. It'll be nice for you to be around women your own age."

"Not lonely, Dad, but I am anxious to see Sadie."

"But she was out at the house only two weeks ago!" said Dad.

Maggie kissed the old man on the cheek and ignored his remark.

"Now, how does the hat look? Mum let me borrow it." Maggie tilted her head in several positions so Dad could get the full benefit of it.

"Come on, what do you think?"

"You look a treat, Maggie."

In Willoughby, with exception to the bank and doctor's office, most businesses combined services. The sign on the Blackburn Hotel declared it also provided ales, tearoom and light meals. Foster's Mercantile housed the Post Office and local newspaper while Samuel Gibson's, livery and blacksmith, offered metal repairs and tool sharpening services. The barber and dentist were one and the same man but Dad didn't think he was much good at either.

"Don't forget to drop off the list of supplies at Foster's, Maggie. I'll pick them up before I meet you tomorrow. Think I'll go to Blackburn's for a pint first and drive out to the Stoddard place this afternoon. He's got a couple of nice ewes I want to take a look at while I'm here. Have a nice time with Sadie and don't tell Mum… about the pint I mean!" Dad put his finger to the side of his nose and laughed. "See you outside Doctor Phillips at four o' clock tomorrow. That be alright?"

"Get on with you and have a good time." Maggie gave him a playful nudge and went into Foster's Mercantile where she was immediately descended upon by a group of old friends. She was delighted to be the centre of attention. The talk turned to deliveries as some of the women relayed their own experiences of childbirth.

"Good God, we'll frighten this poor girl to death!" interjected Sadie.

Sadie Blackburn was a tall thin woman of thirty-five. Her short brown hair was sun- streaked. Laugh lines creased the corners of her bright blue eyes. Her skin was deeply tanned. She would have been a plain woman had it not been for her smile. Sadie had never married and had taken over the Blackburn Hotel from her father after he died. The short-sleeved, tan, belted dress she wore, that buttoned down the front, looked cool and comfortable.

"Why don't we go over to my place for tea and a bit of cake?" she said. "We can all have a nice old chinwag and get this girl off her feet."

Next day, at four o'clock Dad was as good as his word, waiting dutifully curbside in front of Doctor Phillips place. He was preoccupied as he rubbed and squeezed his shoulder then held open the car door for Maggie and all her packages.

"That rheumatism playing you up again is it? Why don't you see the Doctor while we're here? Get him to have a look at it for you," said Maggie.

"Nah! What's he going to tell me I don't already know? Had these spells before. Bit of liniment will put it right. Now then, what did the doctor say about my grandchild?"

"Everything's fine. He said I should move into town, in about a fortnight, just to be on the safe side."

Starting out on the drive home the two chatted about their purchases, an upcoming stock auction and the opening of a hairdressers shop on Dinbar Street.

"Do you ever miss Yorkshire?" Maggie asked.

"I suppose so. Mum more than me. We've been out here a long time now but we've adjusted. Course, Mum would have been out here a lot sooner had my brother played his cards right."

Dad had Maggie's full attention.

"You didn't *know*?" he said. "My brother and I fell in love with the same woman."

"No-one ever told me that," said Maggie.

"But it's true! When Mum married me, he up and left. He made a lot of money in the shipping business. Liked what he saw when he came to Australia. Had a vision he could make the sheep business pay. We'd been raised as sheep farmers, so he knew everything there was to know about sheep. The mills in England were clamoring for wool…and mutton was on everybody's table. When he died he left it all to John, the son he felt *he* should have had. He'd roll over in his grave to think Mum and I had ended up under his roof. After I married Mum, he and I, well, we were never close after that."

"Did he ever marry?"

"No."

"I think Mum made the best choice when she picked you!" said Maggie,

"Damn right she did!" The two burst out laughing.

"How did John talk you into moving?" Dad looked sad for a moment. "Well, there was nothing keeping us there in Yorkshire. John couldn't manage the place, here, by himself and I *knew* sheep. The station's made a tidy little profit each year."

"Mum's the quiet one. She never said a thing about your brother."

"And you won't repeat it either," said Dad with mock stern-ness. "Now then, close your eyes for a bit. It's a long drive back."

Maggie leaned back against the seat and closed her eyes. She hadn't been asleep for long when the car jolted slightly and woke her up. She was a little disoriented, after sleeping, but soon realized that the car was going at quite a speed. She smiled and vacantly patted the old man's hand.

"Ease up a bit Dad." When there was no response she turned to look at him. Dad's face was locked in a mask of pain. His eyes stared straight ahead and his mouth was wide open. His hands gripped the steering wheel.

"Dad? What's the matter? What is it?"

In one motion the old man slumped forward and as he did his foot pressed heavily against the accelerator pedal. The car increased its speed as it veered away from the road. Maggie tried to kick Dad's foot off the pedal but couldn't because of her encumbering abdomen. She wrestled to get control of the car but, in her panic turned the wheel too sharply. There was no time to scream. The car rolled over, twice, then bounced right side up in a cloud of dust. The passenger door flew open and a white sunbonnet cart-wheeled down the dusty road.

It was some time before Maggie opened her eyes. She felt dizzy and vomited. Her head hurt and she felt a stickiness in her hair. She couldn't immediately remember what had happened or where she was. As her mind cleared it all came back to her. Dad wasn't in his seat; the glass was gone from the windscreen, the key still in the ignition. Her eyes widened in terror.

"*Dad?*" she screamed but knew he wouldn't answer.

She remembered his face, right before the accident. Maggie tried to lean forward to see if she could see him but a sharp pain, in her lower abdomen, made her catch her breath. She rubbed her hands in circles, gently, over her stomach. There was no movement. Maggie began to cry. After a while she laid her head back and thought about John. Images whirled around in her mind as she recalled the very first time she saw him.

Maggie had been nineteen and working at the Bryson Point Hotel. She'd been fortunate to get a job there as a waitress. It was an elegant hotel with imported marble floors, white pillars, fountains and wing-backed chairs. A quartet of musicians played chamber music for the dinner guests in the evenings. The hotel catered exclusively to the wealthy.

Maggie saw John the moment she came on duty that evening. He was handsome but looked out of place in a tweed jacket, open necked shirt, and slacks. He was in deep conversation with Howard Bryson, owner of the hotel and railroad company. Bryson looked distinguished in a black tuxedo. A man with thinning hair and a waxed moustache, Bryson was well respected as a shrewd businessman. Maggie noticed John's easy confidence. It showed in the way he sat in his chair, his arm hooked over the back, his laughter and animation as he talked.

"Bring that train into Willoughby and I promise you we'll keep it busy full time. It takes too long to take wool and mutton down river to the train. Times are changing, Howard, we have to meet the demands faster and more efficiently," said John.

Howard Bryson liked this young man with his enthusiasm and eye towards the future but it hadn't stopped him from checking all the angles to make sure it was a profitable venture. John took a sip of his beer while Bryson coddled an aged Scottish whiskey.

"So, have I come on a fool's errand?"

"No, John. I'll bring the train into Willoughby. Not because you talked me into it, mind, but because my banker tells me there's a lot of money to be made." John stood up so quickly he almost tipped his chair over.

The two men shook hands. Maggie, not wanting to interrupt the conversation, held back a moment. When she thought the time was right she hurried to the table.

"May I take your order now, sir?" she said and focused her attention on the older gentleman. "I uh, I'll have the roast beef, Maggie, and another whisky."

"I'll bring you the poached salmon and some water."

"Then why in the hell did you ask if you could take my order if all I can have is poached salmon and water? Aw, Maggie, just this once, the doctor won't even know. It's only Gout!"

Maggie turned her back on Bryson and looked at John.

"And have you decided, sir?"

John scrutinized the waitress very carefully while she was talking to Bryson. He admired her well-defined figure, the slenderness of her neck and the way her hair was caught up at the nape of her neck. John committed to memory every detail of the woman who turned and stood before him. His intense gaze heightened the colour on Maggie's face. He made her feel as though she didn't have a stitch of clothes on.

"I'm a meat and potatoes man, myself," said John. "What would you recommend or do I have to have the salmon and water too?"

"Roast beef or the mutton, sir." Maggie maintained her coolness.

"I'll have the mutton."

"Good choice, sir, and shall I bring another beer with that?" She poised the pencil over her pad and waited.

"Yes, that sounds good, thank you."

Maggie found John's gaze insolent and reflected her agitation by trying to snatch the menu from his hand. John hung onto it for a second or two before letting it go, then turned his attention to Bryson…setting Maggie free from his gaze. In due time she brought back the plates, carefully laying one plate before Bryson and almost slapping the plate down in front of John…splattering a little mint sauce on his jacket.

Maggie rushed to remove the sauce, before it stained, with a white linen serviette.

"I'm so sorry, sir, forgive me," said Maggie, scrubbing at the spot. John enjoyed the closeness of her as she dabbed at his jacket. When she looked up at John he was smiling only inches from her face. She threw the serviette in his lap and left. "Hmmm", said Bryson. "I think you made her a little angry."

"She'll have her whole life to get over it after we're married."

Howard laughed loudly. "A waitress you've only just met?"

"I don't care if she is a waitress. I'm going to marry that girl."

"Well, lad, I might have something to say about that."

"You won't even miss her."

"Don't be too sure …she's my granddaughter!"

"The waitress?"

"A cook's helper *and* a maid. Maggie badgered me for almost a year to give her a job here. I didn't want to but I finally gave in on the condition she start at the bottom and work her way up. Good girl is Maggie."

Maggie felt herself coming around. Blood, from the wound on her head, had soaked the lace collar of her dress. The intense contraction was accompanied by a gush of water. "Oh, God, not out here…not now" she said and braced herself against the seat until the contraction ended.

Maggie was vaguely aware of a presence standing next to the car. "Help me," she whispered. "*Please…* help me." She didn't hear the tribal staff as it slid away from where it had been propped against the car. She was pulled out of her seat and screamed in pain.

Henry picked her up and carried Maggie back along the dusty road. "Car won't start, Missus, but I'll get you back…don't you worry." Henry's bare, feet, padded down the dirt road back to Willoughby. He leaned back in order to carry his burden. Maggie's eyes opened, for a moment, then closed. "Henry, you're *here*?"

"Yes, Missus. I am… supposed to be… *here*."

CHAPTER SIX
Arrivals and Departures

The morning had gone quickly yet John had not been able to get Maggie out of his mind. Sitting on the porch rocker, smoking a cigarette and checking his pocket watch for the fifth time, he was relieved to hear the sound of, what he at first thought was the car.

"Is that them?" asked Mum from inside the kitchen.

John suddenly recognized the rhythmic thudding of horse hooves.

"No Mum, I think it's Ed Tindall." He flicked his cigarette away and walked towards the rider. Mum came out on the porch, drying her hands on a towel.

"John, you'd better come quick… you too Mrs. Reynolds." Ed Tindall was out of breath from the hard ride. His eyes focused on John. "There's been an accident. It's your Dad…and…and Maggie…just outside of town. It's really bad mate!"

John didn't recall how he got to Willoughby that night. He noticed the small group of people, gathered outside Doctor Phillip's house, and was angry at the pity he saw in their eyes. He pushed them aside and made his way inside. Sadie Blackburn stood between him and the door to the small, four bed, room that served as a hospital.

"John, wait a minute," said Sadie placing both hands against his chest to stop him from entering the room. He pulled her hands away, his eyes fixed on the door behind her.

"Listen to me!" Sadie demanded.

"Ed already told me, Dad's had a heart attack, he's dead. Now let me by, I want to see Maggie."

"I wish to God I wasn't the one to be telling you this." Sadie's lips trembled uncontrollably.

"Tell me *what*!"

"They've both... gone," she whispered. John looked at her in disbelief and Sadie put her arms around him. Gripping the back of his shirt in both fists she pulled him to her as she cried.

"You're lying!" John said, and set Sadie aside. He flung open the door and entered the room. Two of the beds held forms covered loosely with white sheets. John saw Maggie's hand. It hung down from the edge of the bed. The plain gold wedding ring he'd placed on her finger seemed large on her pale hand. John tore back the sheet.

It was as if the ground shook from within and an energy built up in the bowels of a volcano. So it was with John Reynolds. An inhuman roar of rage and grief spewed from the depths of him as his world tore apart and his heart broke.

Mum stood behind her son, crying softly, as a woman does who has known sorrow before. One of the women put her arm around her shoulders and led her to a chair.

An hour passed and Doctor Phillips spoke to John. "They'd only just left town. Maggie was still alive, for a while, but there was nothing anyone could have done for her. If it hadn't been for that bloke who works for you we'd have lost the baby too. I'm so...sorry John. Let me take you to see your daughter?"

"No. I want to be with Maggie," said John, his voice low and controlled.

"I know you do," Doctor Phillips said gently, "but let the womenfolk do what has to be done, first."

"Did she say anything? Did Maggie say anything before she...she died?"

"Yes. She made me write it down." Doctor Phillips handed John a piece of folded paper. The handwritten note ended with, "Tell John I love him more."

Maggie lay on clean sheets. She'd already been washed and laid out, arms crossed over her chest. Someone had dressed her in a pink cotton shift. Not a colour she would have chosen to wear, thought John. Her young fresh face looked only asleep.

There was no visible evidence of trauma. Her chestnut bright hair, newly brushed, had been fanned out across the pillow. John traced his finger across her lips then ran his hand down the flatness of her stomach where the baby should have been. He looked towards the adjoining bed, at the sheet that covered his father, and thought about how unreal this all was to him.

John kissed Maggie's lips expecting any moment she'd open her eyes and put her arms around his neck.

Outside, he could hear the bustle and noise of Willoughby beginning the normal routines of the day. He walked to the window and wondered how everything could possibly go on, without missing a beat, while inside the room his whole world had come to a standstill.

John hadn't been aware of Mum in the room, until she whispered, "John, leave me alone with your Dad for a moment, will you?"

Not able to trust himself to speak, afraid he'd break down again, he left the room and closed the door quietly behind him. Mum pulled back the sheet and stared at her husband's face. She placed her hand on his cheek. "I thought losing a child was the worst thing a woman could go through," she said and sighed deeply. "It isn't, you know. Losing the man you love…that's the worst thing. I loved you so much and I don't think…" her face screwed up with fresh tears. "I don't think I ever told you that."

It had been three months since John buried Maggie and his father in the family plot near a grove of Acacia trees. In the branches, twittering green budgerigars looked like bright exotic flowers as they flapped and spread their wings to keep cool.

"Come back to the house, son," said old Mrs. Reynolds. John hadn't been aware of her presence until she stood beside him and spoke. Mum folded her arms and looked at the two mounds of soil. There were no headstones; the ground had to settle first. She glanced at one other grave, that of her husband's brother. The man who had brought them here. Mum thought back to the little girl she'd left behind in England; lost to diphtheria over forty years ago. "It's not good for you to be out here so much." John resented the intrusion. "Leave me be, Mum."

"You keep coming up here every day. It's no use, love, she's gone and so's your dad. We've got to move forward."

John, whose back had been towards his mother, turned and shouted, "Move *forward*? I don't even have a reason to get up in the morning! God's truth, Mum, Dad was an old man but Maggie…where's the sense in it? Tell me that if you can.

"I don't want to hear that kind of talk from you!" said the old woman. "Just got to get on with things, that's all. I miss them too…but we have a sheep station to run and you have a daughter to raise. Lots of work to keep a body busy. I want some help boxing up Dad and Maggie's clothes. House needs a good clean out."

"Mum, I didn't mean to…" John didn't get to finish his apology as his mother had already walked off towards the house. He followed her.

From somewhere in the house a baby cried and John walked directly towards the sound and looked down at Alice who lay in the cradle Dad had made. She'd been crying for quite a while and had the back of her fist stuck in her mouth. He picked her up and held her at arm's length. She immediately stopped crying but still had dry sobs from all the exertion. She had her mother's fair skin and what little hair she had was strawberry blonde, fine, and curled up on top of her head like a rooster's comb.

"Wait your hurry, Madam, I'm coming, I'm coming!" fussed Mum shaking milk onto her inner wrist from the rubber teat of a glass baby bottle. She took the baby from John.

"There now." She sat down and cuddled the baby to her. Alice scratched her nails on the raised print of the boat shaped bottle as she sucked the warm milk. Her father watched and wondered why he felt nothing for his child.

Later that night, unable to sleep, John began to clear out Maggie's things. He pulled out drawers, emptied them onto the bed then stuffed everything into pillowcases. In the wardrobe he stopped at the sight of Maggie's blue candlewick dressing gown, the scent of her still lingered in the soft folds of the fabric.

John noticed a small, square, biscuit tin tucked in a corner of the top shelf of the wardrobe. He'd never seen the box before. He took it down, sat on the bed, and sorted through the contents. There were several letters, he'd written to Maggie, tied with yellow satin ribbon, a birth certificate, telegrams from the army, no doubt to notify her that he was missing, and two cream bonded letters addressed to him and forwarded by his regiment.

One of the letters had been opened. '*My Dearest John*' it began. John's heart jumped to his throat and the box fell from his hand. Maggie had known…about Phoebe Mannington.

As he sat in his Father's chair, John poured out his guilt and remorse to Mum. She sat quietly for a moment.

"I told Maggie to throw those letters away and think n' more about it," she said and leaned forward in her chair when Alice stirred. Mum tapped her foot steadily on the rocker of the cradle, until the baby went back to sleep, then leaned back and continued knitting the yoke of a white lacy jacket she was making for Alice.

"Jesus Christ! She told *you* about it? Why didn't Maggie say something to me? I loved her…I still love her. I wouldn't have hurt her for the world. Maggie must have thought I…"

"Rubbish!" said Mum. "She thought no such thing! She *knew* you loved her. 'If he brings it up then you talk about it,' I told her, 'but if he doesn't then it must not have mattered so leave it be'. Men go off to war, John, and don't come back until the war's over. Sometimes that takes years. Women wait. When it's over we hope we can pick up where we left off and neither talks about the time between. It's just the way things are."

Mum unpicked two rows of knitting to retrieve a dropped stitch.

"It didn't mean anything!" John said. "I'd have told her that."

"Now't you can do now. Just got to get on with things, I say. The war's taken enough from us already. You've got Alice. She's a part of you and Maggie. Think about *her*."

John, still with the crumpled letters in his hand, got up and kissed the top of his Mother's head. "You're the only solid ground in my life right now Mum." He glanced briefly at Alice before he left the room. Not a woman to ever drop a stitch, Mum put her knitting on her lap, laid her head back and stared at Dad's chair. She wondered if God would forgive her for the lies she just told, and thought about dear sweet Maggie who kept the letters a secret from *everyone.*

Next morning there was a cry from the kitchen. "John come quick, *hurry!*" John came crashing through the kitchen door expecting to see a grease fire on the stove or something of equal emergency.

"What is it Mum, what's wrong?" he asked, a little irritated to be called away from his chores for no apparent reason.

Mum held out one of Phoebe's letters. "Nosey old woman that I am, I opened the other letter. There's a child John… your child!"

"What are you talking about, woman!" he said and grabbed the piece of paper. The words leapt off the page as Phoebe related her desperate situation and confrontation with James.

Dropping into a chair at the, scrubbed wood, kitchen table John ran his fingers through his hair and re-read the letter, then got up and left the house, slamming the door behind him.

He walked to the cemetery and stood over Maggie's grave.

"*Why*? Why didn't you tell me you knew?" he shouted. "She didn't mean anything Maggie…I swear to God." John paced back and forth. "I should have told you about Phoebe. I knew nothing about this child, Maggie…I swear. How am I supposed to live with this? S'truth! You're the only one I ever loved, Maggie. I've made such a bloody mess of things."

Where before the air was still, a soft breeze stirred in the branches of the trees. It brushed against John's cheek and felt warm across the back of his neck. Then it was gone as suddenly as it came. John stood for a moment before striding back to the house.

Mum had been watching for her son, from the window. As John came into the house and sat back on the kitchen chair, she reached into the back of the larder for a bottle of rum. She'd kept it put by for a toast after the baby's christening, or as Dad had put it, "To wet the baby's head." But, with the accident…she poured a generous quantity into a glass and slid it towards her son.

"What will you do?"

John knocked back the rum in one gulp. "I'm going to England on the next boat."

CHAPTER SEVEN
Return to Baden Hall

It had been more than five years since John Reynolds stood on the steps of Baden Hall. Thomas opened the great door and recognized the tall man in the brown tweed jacket, open necked shirt and grey slacks. He thought how foreign his suntanned skin looked against the drab English climate.

"Mr. Reynolds, sir, you're expected... follow me, please." Reynolds was shown into the library where James Mannington sat, rigidly, in his wheelchair. He was thinner than John remembered. His pallid skin and pinched expression made him look older than his years. He was dressed somewhat like John except for a white cravat, knotted and tucked in, at his throat.

"Surprised to see you had the gall to show your face here, Reynolds... you can stay Thomas," he added as he saw the old butler start to leave.

"I'm here to see Phoebe, not ..." John began. James didn't allow him to finish.

"If I was the man I used to be you'd be picking yourself up off the floor. It's only for Phoebe's sake that I've allowed you into my house. I wasn't certain I'd ever have the opportunity to say what I think of you, Reynolds. You were a guest in my home, someone I thought of as a friend, yet you took advantage of my hospitality. Do you have any idea what the ramifications were of what you did? Phoebe and I haven't spoken in years, not since..."

"Just hear me out first, James. I'm not denying that what I did was wrong but I'm here to take full responsibility for the child. I will make things right."

"So...it's a sense of duty that brings you here...how honorable of you," said James and saluted theatrically.

"Where's Phoebe?"

"Oh, she's here. Came in on the first train this morning. She's Mrs. George Sinclair now. Tell me, (James leaned his head back against the chair and closed his eyes) was your wife a good sport about all this? Did she forgive you?"

John turned to leave the room in search of Phoebe, his jaw set and fists clenched. James called after him. "Don't worry, Reynolds, I cleaned up the little mess you left behind. The boy was put out for adoption." He gloated, satisfied that his barb had reached its target.

John let go of the doorknob but stood frozen in place while he absorbed the impact of what he'd just heard. He turned to face James. "Phoebe would never have done such a thing. You're lying!"

"Couldn't have the little bastard dirtying up our family titles now could I?"

John felt hot and inside his head it was as though a rubber band had snapped. In two strides he was across the room and had almost lifted James, by the front of his jacket, out of the wheelchair. Thomas crossed the room and held Reynolds arm back just before his fist could make contact. James hadn't made a move to defend himself. He just laughed while John stood breathing heavily in anger, then his laughter turned to rage.

"Thomas…throw him out!" James bellowed.

"No! Captain Reynolds will be staying," said a voice John recognized. He looked over his shoulder and there, in the doorway, stood Phoebe. Her hair was bobbed in a short, almost oriental, style. The light beige dress had the dropped waistline and short skirt that was fashionable for the new woman of the 1920's. Low –heeled 'T- strap' shoes and a string of pearls with matching earrings completed the look of expensive elegance.

"Hello John," she said. Her voice sounded cold and flat. "How good of you to come. Please sit down. Thomas, get me a gin and tonic will you? Well, it doesn't sound like much has changed, James!" John noticed Phoebe wore meticulously applied make up and was a little unsteady in her gait.

"Thomas, I told you to throw him out!" ordered Mannington, the vein in his neck extended and his jaw jutted out.

"Oh, shut-up, James," Phoebe said in a bored tone. "Well John Reynolds, you're back but, I'm afraid, you're too late." She took a sip of her drink.

"Look, I didn't know until…"

"Such a beautiful baby." Phoebe's eyes looked vacant as she recalled the child. John fell silent.

"Do you have children?" Phoebe asked.

"Yes. " John cast his eyes downward. "I have a daughter."

"You have a son too!" Phoebe said, sarcastically, "somewhere."

"If you'd just let me explain! I didn't know! You've got to believe me, Phoebe, I just didn't know." John paused. "And why in the hell did you give him up for adoption?"

"Why in the hell didn't you tell me you were married? Do you think I wanted to give up my baby? You don't understand how it was."

"Just tell me where to start looking. I'll find him." John had Phoebe's full attention.

"You'll never find him now," said James. "It was years ago. You can't walk in here and stir everything back up again. You ruined my sister's life."

"No, James," Phoebe said sharply, "You and I did that."

"What are you talking about? He was the one who…"

"I could live with what he did, James. From the moment my baby was taken from me I grieved for him as though he'd died in my arms that day."

"But you signed the paper yourself."

"What choice did I have?" Phoebe shouted back.

"I don't have to listen to this!" said James and, merely to make some sort of statement than have a direction in mind, spun his wheels with the heels of his hands.

"But you *will* listen, James. If John thinks he can find my son then I want to hear what he has to say." Phoebe stood in front of the wheelchair preventing her brother's retreat.

"You're drunk!"

"Oh, I've been drunk for years James. It's the only way I could manage to live with myself!"

"I was doing what was best for everyone. You agreed to it. I saw to it that you married well and had everything you could possibly want. I'm not the villain in all this…he is." James pointed his finger at John yet never took his eyes off his sister.

"He left you... pregnant. *He* didn't see the state you were in. I gave you the best care money could buy. Where was *he* when you needed help?"

"Will someone just listen to me!" shouted John.

Phoebe backed away from the wheelchair and handed her empty glass to Thomas.

"I wasn't in any condition to make decisions for myself!" she said, ignoring John's comment. "None of what happened was what I wanted and if there's any chance of getting my son back..."

James didn't answer.

"Damn you!" Phoebe shouted angrily. "You used to be a good man, James, but look at yourself; you're neither use nor ornament! I've got news for you. Like so many others the war left you with a handicap, but it was your mind that turned you into an invalid. You bloody well gave up! I know, for a fact, you haven't left this house, once, since the Army sent you home. Your whole world has been reduced to this room!"

"And how would you know that? You haven't set foot in this house for years!" Thomas looked uncomfortable. James glared at him.

"I'm asking for your help, James. You have the contacts. My son is the only Mannington left, or hasn't that occurred to you?" The clock on the mantle ticked loudly in the silence that followed.

"Do you still love him?" James nodded his head in the direction of Reynolds. Phoebe knelt beside her brother and took his hand.

"No, James, but once I thought I did. John never loved me. He was lonely and I wanted to comfort him. I was young. The baby was the only part that was real. I have a husband who loves me. I haven't been much of a wife to him but I could be if I had my son back. Don't you see?"

James didn't reply. The room was silent as each person reflected on what had been said. Phoebe stood up while James pivoted his chair and looked out of the window. The old butler held his breath.

"Please James," pleaded Phoebe. "Not a day's gone by I haven't thought about him. You and I never talked about it after..." Her voice trailed off.

"Why didn't you just go and get the boy back, Phoebe. Why did you wait?" asked John.

"What could I do alone? Then I met George, a Member of Parliament. There was his career to think about. I only told him, about the child, when your letter arrived. He said I should have told him, he'd have understood and that he loved me. I'd been so terrified of what would happen if he ever found out. George said it wouldn't have made any difference and that he'd have raised the boy as his own." She turned to her brother.

"What irony there is in that, James, for all our secrets it didn't matter."

"My position hasn't changed. Leave well enough alone, Phoebe. I won't help you," said James and made for the door.

"Then damn you!" shouted Phoebe. "Go and shut yourself in your room and rot in the hell you've made for yourself!"

John plunged his hands deep into his trouser pockets. "This isn't getting us anywhere," he said. He and Phoebe talked, for a moment about their lives and what had happened since they last met.

Thomas soon returned to the room. Phoebe nodded her head towards him for another drink.

"I'll start at Sacred Heart and work my way from there. It would have helped if there'd been something on the birth certificate," said John.

"I just couldn't bring myself to. It was hard enough giving him up."

"Pardon for the interruption, Miss," said Thomas. "There was a name on the birth certificate...*mine*."

"What are you talking about, Thomas?" said Phoebe.

"I gave him my name. *I* signed the birth certificate." Phoebe wracked her brain. She never knew Thomas by any other name than Thomas.

"Your Grandmother named me when I was born Miss...after an Irish saint."

"What name did you put on the birth certificate?" John asked.

"Declan Mannington Thomas." Phoebe was speechless, for a moment, as she absorbed this information. "Thomas, why didn't you ever say?"

Thomas lowered his head but did not reply.

"Well, it'll give me something to go on," said John and turned Phoebe to face him.

"Look, I can't change what's past, wish to God that I could. I can promise you this much though, Phoebe, I will find the boy!"

The look of determination on John Reynolds face made Phoebe believe him.

CHAPTER EIGHT
Mrs. Wilson

It was late in the day when John stood in front of the ministry building, in London. It had once been a grand residence in Georgian times but now looked sorely neglected. Pigeons fluttered onto the slate rooftop then jostled for roosting positions in the last of the evening light.

John was directed to a darkly paneled room. The door was open. On the walls hung oil paintings of stone-faced benefactors of the establishment. An ornate hooded fireplace had cold ash in the grate. The room smelled of polish mixed with the mustiness of damp wood. Even in broad daylight John suspected little light filtered through the soot–grimed windows.

There was something very familiar about the young woman sitting behind the oak desk at the back of the room. John tapped on the glass of the open door.

"You can lock up in a minute, Fred, I've almost finished," said the woman, pre-occupied with a sheaf of papers. She had a fresh scrubbed natural look about her.

Dark curls pinned up, on top of her head, were starting to fall over one eye. She looked up and was startled to see it wasn't Fred who was standing there.

"Oh! Forgive me; I thought you were the janitor."

"I'm here to… see… Mrs. Wilson. My name's John Reynolds," John said haltingly as he tried to place where he'd seen this woman before. She indicated for him to sit on a rickety chair and brushed a stray curl out of her eyes with the back of her hand.

"I'm Mrs. Wilson but you can call me Louise. We're not formal here," she said pleasantly.

"You're not going to believe this," said John, "but we *have* met before… in France." He struggled to perch his frame on the shaky chair.

"It was when you pushed your hair out of your eyes with the back of your hand that I remembered. You were the field nurse who bandaged my head."

"There were so many soldiers," Louise said sadly. "I took great care not to know their names but I do remember the faces...every one of them and... you're still a long way from home!" She smiled. "Now, how can I help you?"

"I'm trying to find my son. He was given up for adoption about ten years ago. I want him back."

"Ten years! It'll be impossible to find him after that length of time." It was usually the mother, who came asking for a child's return...not the father, thought Louise.

Fred, the janitor, put his head around the door. Louise took the hint.

"Look Mr. Reynolds, I don't mean to give you the push but it's past office hours, it's getting dark and I have a tram to catch. Come back tomorrow and I'll help you fill out a form." She got up to leave. John stood up and slapped his hand down on the desk in front of Louise.

"Look! I've been sent from one agency to the next. I know you're in a rush to get home to Mr. Wilson and all the little Wilsons," he hissed through his teeth, "but give me a minute here will you? Convents, institutions, orphanages... I've had the grand tour!" John blinked rapidly, stopped himself and stepped back.

"I didn't mean to startle you, I..."

"I'm not a woman who startles easily, Mr. Reynolds!" she said indignantly.

"I'm sorry. I didn't mean to take it out on *you*. It's just been a very long day and I'm dog- tired. I haven't eaten since this morning and I still have to look for a place to stay. I'll...look I'll just come back tomorrow and fill out the form." John turned to leave. Louise felt pity for the man.

"Wait... there's a pub down the street, 'The Ploughman'. They have clean rooms, good food and it's close enough to The Agency here. Just let me get my coat on and I'll take you." John was surprised at her change of heart. "Thank you," he said.

"Don't be too quick to thank me, you're treating me to Shepherd's pie and a glass of port at the pub. We can talk there."

"What about your tram?" inquired John?

Louise sighed. "I'll catch a later one."

John moved quickly to help her on with her coat then strode across the room to hold the door for her.

"There's no need to overdo it, Mr. Reynolds, I said I'd help you!"

"John," he said and grinned. "Call me John, we're not formal here, you know."

Louise gave him a side- glance. "Hmm," she said pulling on her gloves.

It had been raining on and off all day. The street lamps made halos of light on the wet cobbled street and the slight smell of chimney smoke tainted the cold Autumn air. The Tudor pub had whitewashed bricks with black beams embedded in the walls and swirled 'bottle-bottomed' windowpanes. As John and Louise entered the old tavern the warmth of the blazing, open-hearth, fire rushed to greet them. There was a smell of stale ale, wet woolen clothes and pipe smoke.

Louise found a high-backed settle at a table near the fire. It was too early for most of the regulars but a few patrons sat at the bar talking. Louise laughed, amused at the difficulty John was having with his height and the low beamed ceiling. After the second bump on the forehead he maneuvered carefully and walked in a stooped position to avoid any further contact. John and Louise chatted, comfortably, as though old friends. He told her about his home in Australia, the loss of his wife and father, about his daughter, Alice, and how difficult it had been to feel anything for her or anyone else. He told her of his years in the war, his loneliness for Maggie, about Phoebe and his search for a child he never knew existed until recently.

Louise turned her glass and studied the wet rings it made on the dark polished wood table.

"I don't know why I'm baring my soul like this. I don't expect you to understand," said John. They both fell silent for a while.

"There isn't a Mr. Wilson," Louise said, flatly, as she looked into her glass, "and there aren't any children. My husband, David, was killed in France."

"Oh! S'truth. I didn't know. I'm sorry I said…"

"It's all right, you weren't to know. I couldn't move forward and there was nothing to go back to. So, I volunteered as a field nurse in France. Somehow, I felt closer to where David had been… useful at least."

"So, now the war is over and you work with children?"

"I was needed here. The war left many father-less children. Mothers had little means to support them. I'm not just talking about illegitimate children, John. Many regiments were from the same county. If that battalion was wiped out it wouldn't be uncommon to find a whole village with nobody but women, children and old men. It was a struggle for mothers to put food on the table. Whatever the reason, shame, family pressure or economics the children were handed over to us by the hundreds. You say your son is nearly ten?"

"By now he would be."

"If he's been adopted there'll be a different name. One thing in your favour, though, is that The Agency keeps very detailed records. You can start tomorrow."

"Me?"

"Well, I don't have time to go through all that paperwork. I can help but you'll have to do most of it." Louise looked thoughtful for a moment then said, "If it isn't rude of me to ask? How come a poor sheep farmer can afford to take so much time away from the farm?"

"In Australia it's called a station! I said I was a sheep farmer...I didn't say I was poor."

"But you live with your parents?"

"No. They live with me. My uncle immigrated to Australia. When he died I inherited his place in Willoughby. The house was far too big for me so, since we had no other family in England, we moved. My Father was the best sheep farmer in the Dales of Yorkshire. Big demand for Australian mutton and wool. The town's prospering and so are my neighbours. Good people in Willoughby."

"I envy you family, I have none."

The days flew past. Every day John searched through lists of names and records and in the evenings he and Louise walked or chatted over a meal at 'The Ploughman'. John knew that Louise was aware that something was happening between them. He'd noticed where once conversation had been familiar and comfortable, Louise now seemed embarrassed if he looked at her or happened to stand too closely.

"What are you afraid of?" John asked her, over drinks at the pub.

She nervously fiddled with that lock of hair that always strayed across her eyes. John reached across the table and swept the wayward curl back from her face. He traced his fingers along her cheek. Louise got up, abruptly, and pushed her way through the incoming regulars and out onto the street. John was right behind her. Louise was unsure which way to go in her confusion. John said nothing just pulled her into his arms and kissed her.

The next day Louise handed John another stack of papers, ledgers and dockets.

"Are these the last of them?" he complained.

"Not by any means!" she said, and left. Towards lunchtime Louise popped her head around the door. "I've made you a cup of tea and I'll split my sandwich with you," she said. John was preoccupied with some papers. The look on his face told her something was wrong.

"John, what is it?" He looked up and said incredulously, "All these children were sent abroad."

"I know, Canada, Australia and some of the brightest to Rhodesia."

John looked at her in astonishment. "It says here they were to be trained as farm laborers and domestic servants? Money changed hands when they were turned over. These children were...sold!" He looked intently at Louise hoping she would explain to him how wrong he was.

She laughed. "Don't be ridiculous. You make it sound like slavery! The children are sent to dormitories in England and Wales, They attend school, are taught cleanliness and skills that will help them to fit into the communities they're to go to. The foster parents save a little pocket money for them each month in trade for the work."

"And if they're adopted?"

"Well, look you're making it sound as though it's something terrible."

"Cheap farm labor...or even better... free. A workforce of children. You said the brightest may to go to Rhodesia. Why?"

"They'd live a privileged life, be sent to the best boarding schools."

"Of course! White English children being primed to install in a later British government!" Louise didn't catch the sarcasm in his voice.

"Yes, good homes in British colonies, a wonderful start in life, away from the poverty they'd have experienced here."

"What you're telling me is that my son was sent to one of these countries?"

"Yes!"

"Don't you see something wrong with that, Louise? Selling a man's children while he's defending England. What in God's name do you think we were fighting for?" John shouted.

Louise looked shocked at his implication.

"What alternative was there? And they weren't... being... sold!" she yelled back. "My God you're a frustrating man!" She turned and left. John stood silent, for a moment, absorbing the full measure of his discovery.

The air was thick with tension between the two but they continued to work together exchanging pieces of information when they had to. One morning Louise handed John a piece of paper.

"A telegram for you." John read the words out loud. "*Declan Mannington Thomas*. S'truth it's him! Date of birth is right but what do these numbers, next to his name, mean?"

"Identification of child and intended country, let me see that," said Louise. John handed over the telegram. By the end of the day Louise had the information she was looking for.

"He was sent to Australia, John. In your own back yard, so to speak."

"Australia's a big country," he replied. Louise turned to walk away but John grabbed her arm.

"Listen, tomorrow's Saturday, let me take you somewhere special for dinner...to celebrate. I've not changed my mind, about what I think of all this, but it wasn't you I should have been yelling at. What do you say, Louise, truce?"

"I already have plans for Saturday night. I'm going to a party."

"Who with?"

"You! I just wasn't sure if I wanted to ask you. I was angry."

"I know."

"Well, you made me feel as though I'd personally shipped children into hell. I saw this as a wonderful opportunity for them, but the truth is I don't know what happens to them once they reach their destination point. I haven't been able to sleep, thinking about it, so I'm going to Australia with the next batch of migrant children. I *will* find your son. The ship leaves in five days. Being with The Agency I have enough authority to give me access to information and with my nursing experience I'll be useful on the journey."

"Then I'm going with you. I'll book passage on the same ship."

The next evening John picked Louise up outside her boarding house.

He hadn't noticed, before, how beautiful she was but in the lamplight her dark hair shone and her brown eyes looked like velvet. Ringlets of curls were piled up on the side of her head and caught in a glittering diamond-like comb. She wore a long black coat over a well-fitting, ivory, satin gown and matching shoes. Her pear-shaped drop earrings matched the necklace and hair ornament.

"David's tuxedo fits you beautifully," she said. John must have stared at her too long.

"What is it…a smudge on my face…what?"

"No, it's…n' nothing", he stammered.

"Are you sure?"

"Come on," John said gruffly and steered her towards the hackney cab.

"Where is this place?" he asked.

"In the country, belongs to Elizabeth Ames. It's her birthday. She was a nurse in France with me and a good friend. Lost her husband to mustard gas."

'The Manse' was a beautiful old manor house that overlooked the river. Lights shone from every window. It had well maintained grounds and centuries old oak trees. A courtyard, at the front, displayed a statue of Pan who soundlessly played his pipes as he danced across a rectangular shaped lily-pond. As they entered the hallway, with its rose and indigo Persian rug and elegant gilt mirror they could hear strains of Debussy's Clair De Lune being played on a piano.

"Bit ostentatious, isn't it?" said Elizabeth Ames directing her comment towards John and giving Louise a hug.

"Heard all about you," said Elizabeth. She was a stout jolly woman with an easy smile and strong handshake.

"Want you to meet Archie Tyler, John. He's a flying ace; friend of mine. You'll find him most interesting." Elizabeth introduced the two men then bustled Louise off to the cloakroom

Archie was a small runt of a man with a moustache. He was dressed in uniform and smoked a sweet smelling pipe.

"So, you're an 'Aussie?' I've a lot of respect for you boys. Proud to know you," Archie said and held out his hand. John noticed how badly the man's hand shook.

"Oh, don't mind that, they tell me it'll go away in time."

"How many did you shoot down?" John asked.

"Most of them I didn't shoot down…dropped rocks on them! I'd put a few good sized rocks on the floor of the cockpit before each flight. When I ran out of ammunition I'd lob the rocks right through the thin skins of the planes. Aviators secret weapon, lad. Downed a few that way," said Archie. "That's how I got my medals." He indicated the multiple decorations on his jacket by tapping his pipe stem against them.

"Who would have ever guessed that bowling a cricket ball, as a boy, would come in so handy!" said Archie.

Both men laughed.

"So, what are you doing now?" said John.

"Helping Elizabeth while I recover from the tremors. The soldiers you see here tonight have recovered physically, as much as they're going to, but emotionally they're not ready to face family and friends back home, so they stay here."

John looked more closely at the other guests and saw that many were indeed impaired in some manner, but not all the disabilities were apparent. Men and women chatted and smoked cigarettes like at any other party.

"After a while," said Archie, "the family sees the man, not just the disability. That's what this place is all about. A soldier needs to know if his wife or fiancé can accept the disfigurement of a burn or missing limb. Better to be rejected here on neutral ground. In this setting they can visit and re-connect with the people they were before the war. It's not quite so hard this way. Elizabeth's idea."

"But you seem fine?"

"I am. I only stay because I've had my eye on Elizabeth for some time. I'm almost ready to make my move." Archie winked. Here comes that young lady of yours," said Archie.

Louise tucked her hand in John's arm and said, "They're playing a waltz and I haven't danced in years. Do you know how to dance?"

"I do," he said and swept her out onto the floor. His grip was firm and he twirled her around smoothly.

"Impressive." she said against his shoulder. "Looking down at you on the stretcher, that day, I never would have guessed we'd run into each other again. Don't you wonder about that, John?"

On a different thread of thought, as often happens in communication between men and women, John said, "I seem to remember you as taller.

From my perspective on the ground it's understandable…but when I saw you in your office I was surprised to see how…"

"Short I was? Is that what you were going to say! You think I'm short?" She moved away and looked up at him. "I'm of average height for a woman," she said indignantly. John pulled her back close.

"You didn't let me finish…how beautiful you were. There's nothing average about you, Louise Wilson."

The music stopped and Louise turned to go but John tightened his hold around her waist and pulled her back to him. The moment became an uncomfortable eternity for Louise.

"Shall we just go outside so you can kiss me?" she asked breaking the silence.

"Only if I can lead!"

"Where are you two rushing off to," asked Elizabeth.

"Back in a moment," Louise called back. In the courtyard she wrapped her arms around John's neck. His lips were eager and hard against the softness of hers. The intensity of the kiss left them both shaken.

"I didn't think I could feel anything for anyone else after Maggie, but I was wrong," said John. Louise knew exactly what he meant. They'd been no-one of any consequence since David.

"Would your answer be no if I asked you to spend the night with me?" asked Louise.

"No," said John.

"Oh, I see." Louise looked embarrassed. "Well we do have to get an early start tomorrow."

"My answer was no, because I would *not* say no if you invited me to spend the night with you. You didn't listen to your own question." John kissed her again while Pan looked on mischievously.

Elizabeth and Archie watched the two from the window. Archie smiled at Elizabeth. She didn't look at him but said curtly, "And you can get that gleam out of your eye Archie Tyler, the answer is still no!"

CHAPTER NINE
The Voyage

It was a bleak morning at the Southampton dock. Seagulls wheeled and cried in the wake of the returning fishing boats. With ages ranging from four to fourteen, seventy three children stood braced against the cold channel wind; boys in one group and girls in another. A nun, looking like a black and white magpie, in her stiff and heavy habit, rapped out instructions as she held onto her headdress and leaned into the wind.

"Move a little closer to the wall so we can be out of the wind a bit," Sister Theresa said to her charges as she tried to hang onto a clipboard that was bound and determined to take flight. "And when I call your names you're to answer, 'Present'." She looked up to make sure she'd been heard.

"Agnes Crowley?"

"Present."

"Kate Dawson?"

"Present, Sister."

The roster continued to be called until the list was complete.

"Stay together until we get on the ship. You older girls take charge of the little ones. After the photographer has taken your snapshots, put your boarding passes round your necks. " Sister was referring to identification cards hanging by a length of string.

A small fishing vessel lurched and groaned against the ropes that moored it to the capstan while the huge ship, standing ready to board its passengers, held steady against the rough sea. The children watched a regiment of soldiers walk up the wooden boarding plank to the ship. With tin mugs, metal boxes and implements that defied description, clipped to their belts, the soldiers clattered and rattled like gypsy tinkers. Each man carried a rifle, slung across his back, and balanced a duffle-bag across one shoulder.

"It's a bloody oil tanker!" said Private Watkins.

"You were expecting a Cunard Ocean Liner?" yelled the Sergeant, three inches from Watkins face. "Get a move on!"

John gave Louise his hand as she stepped out of the taxi. The driver unloaded their suitcases and boxes. The pair maneuvered down the slippery stone steps to the dock.

"As soon as we get on board, I'll get set up in the dispensary," said Louise.

The photographer, snapping pictures of the children, ordered smiles. After passing the group John slowed his pace and looked back over his shoulder. He was riveted by what he saw. There was something he recognized from a long time ago. In the eyes of the children there was sadness mixed with apprehension. They were leaving behind all that was safe and familiar, knowing in the pit of their stomachs there were terrible things that lie ahead. That was how the soldiers had looked the day they'd left Melbourne to go to war.

"They're afraid," John said.

"Don't be silly. It's an adventure for them, I'm sure they're quite looking forward to it," said Louise.

Kate Dawson noticed the couple and wondered who they were.

Once on board, the Catholic nuns managed to get the children assigned to quarters, reassuring them repeatedly that there was nothing to be concerned about.

The ship severed its ties with the dock and blasted its horn sending the children scattering in frenzy and scurrying under bunks and benches screaming in terror. The first day the ship pitched and rocked as it headed into rough waters. Most of the children and soldiers were violently seasick.

The smart clothes, worn only for travel and the photographer, had been collected, neatly folded and exchanged for some that were more serviceable. They would be loaned out again, at the end of the journey, and then returned to England for the next batch of migrants.

Louise met the man she'd be working with in the dispensary. When she opened the door he was taking off his uniform jacket and placing it on the back of a chair.

"Well," he said, looking Louise up and down. "This trip may not be a total loss after all."

"I'm Louise Wilson, the nurse for the children."

"Jack Porter, ship's doctor, or at least until we get to Gibraltar. So, we'll be working together, I hear." Porter was of medium height with black hair and an olive cast to his skin. He looked more Mediterranean than English. Louise removed her gloves. Jack Porter noticed the wedding ring on her left hand just as John walked into the dispensary.

"Ah! *Mr.* Wilson I presume?"

"No. John Reynolds."

Kate Dawson lay on the bottom bunk, head to toe with another migrant girl and listened to a mouse scurry across the floor. Her hands clasped behind her head she was wide-awake and thinking about her brother, Harry. She'd promised her mother she'd take care of him and felt guilty she'd not been able to keep that promise. Their mother, stricken with tuberculosis, had been taken to a sanitarium. Their father never returned from the war. The Agency collected both children.

Kate, at fourteen, was tall for her age. She had thick russet hair that once hung in a long braid down her back but The Agency had cut it because of too many outbreaks of lice. All girls were given the same short bob with fringe across the forehead. Kate's brown wide-set eyes were her most attractive feature. It was easy to see she was growing up to become a natural beauty.

Living accommodations, on the ship, consisted of a long dormitory-like space and wood planked floors with dark stains of something spilled. Dozens of metal tubes snaked across the low ceiling and down the painted, dirty, walls. The few bunk beds, roughhewn, were bolted down. Some of the girls shared mattresses that lay on the floor.

Kate could see the wooden slats of the bunk above in the faint glow that came from lights on the outer deck of the ship. She turned her face to the wall and thought about sleep. She became aware of a presence next to the bed and turned back over.

A small voice whispered to her, "I'm so cold...my bed's wet." Kate couldn't see the child clearly, but guessed her age to be about four. Kate put out her hand and got up. "It's all right; I'll get you washed up and find something for you to put on, then you can come in bed with us."

"You'll do no such thing!" Kate hadn't heard the nun come into the room. Sister Constance had a soft tread. She was thin and wore round wire- framed glasses on her nose. Her lips were almost nonexistent. She had a sharp tongue and heavy hand with the children. Sister Constance

was a strong believer in discipline and many carried the welts, across the backs of their legs, from her willow cane.

"Sleep in it! It'll be a lesson to you. Back to bed!" she said. "And I'd better not catch you crying about it! You did it... you can lie in it."

"I'll take care of her. It won't be any trouble, Sister," Kate said.

"Mind your business, madam!" the nun said sharply and led the child back to her bed. As soon as she left, Kate was up and tiptoeing across the room.

The warmer weather and smoother seas brought the children out on deck for exercises. The nuns had established routines for prayers, reading, washing and clean up of quarters. Hair was washed with lye soap and rinsed in vinegar to prevent head-lice. The boys were allowed on the upper deck to watch the soldiers practice firing their weapons out to sea. The soldiers did calisthenics, cleaned their guns and equipment, wrote letters home and wiled away some of the time by playing cards.

Into the second week Kate stood at the rail and watched the bow of the ship as it sliced its way through the water causing great arcs of spray as the sea ran from the intrusion. She didn't hear Louise, come up on her, until she spoke.

"You're the Dawson girl aren't you?" said Louise.

"Yes, Mrs. Wilson."

"I've heard about you from some of the other children."

Louise turned, folded her arms and leaned her back against the rail to face Kate.

"I just came out for some air; the dispensary gets a bit stuffy. So, where are you from, Kate?"

"London."

"This must be quite a change for you, then?"

Kate didn't answer.

"A new country, open spaces. It'll be wonderful for you."

"Not to be disrespectful, Mrs. Wilson, but I'm not an orphan like some of the others. I have a family. I shouldn't even be here. My brother, Harry, must be terrified without me."

Louise realized she wasn't speaking to any ordinary child who could be appeased by storybook images of far off lands. "I don't understand. Why were you sent to The Agency if you have parents? "

"Because my mother had…she was ill and was sent to hospital. My Dad didn't come back from the war."

Louise studied the child for a moment. "Oh! I see." There was a long silence before Louise said, "I'm looking for someone to help me in the dispensary. Just some general cleaning up. You're good with the children, they trust you. I'm thinking it might be a good idea to have you there, they'd feel more comfortable with someone they know. What do you think?"

"I'd like that," said Kate.

"Good. Then you can start first thing tomorrow." After discussing the circumstances prior to how Kate ended up at The Agency, Louise understood the maturity and seriousness of the girl and felt a great compassion for her.

"I'd better get back," Kate said. Louise nodded.

Sister Constance stepped out on deck, her black lace-up shoes silent. She didn't see Louise right away, as a column blocked her view, but Sister Constance saw Kate.

"I've been looking for you!" she said, her voice as irritating as a steel knife sliding across a china plate. "Thought I'd find you up here, you skiving little heathen. Idle to the bone is what you are. There's work to be done!" Kate quickened her step.

"You'd better walk a little faster than that, my girl, or I'll lay into you and make the back of your legs smart." The sound of her willow cane swished through the air as she flexed it in a threatening motion. Louise Wilson stepped into view.

Sister Constance, caught in an un-pious act, was unsure what to say next.

"You may go now, Kate," Louise said. After the girl was out of sight, Louise grabbed the cane from the old nun's hand and threw it overboard.

"You won't be attending the children from now on, Sister Constance. Your duties will be confined to that of a domestic nature. I intend to report you to The Agency." The wizened faced nun opened her mouth to say something but thought better of it. She turned on her heel and left.

At the dispensary Kate worked hard. She scrubbed and cleaned everything until it shone. Her compassionate nature dominated any revulsion to the sight of vomit or gashes.

At the end of Kate's first day, Louise rolled her sleeves down and said. "How about we have a cup of tea?" Louise and Kate talked easily. There were many chats over a cup of tea at the end of each day. Most of the children were brought into the dispensary with colds, splinters, bumps or sore throats. Only two cases were out of the ordinary. The first was a girl, aided by another, who came into the dispensary with eyes wide with terror and face ashen.

"What is it?" said Louise.

The girl brought a towel out from under her dress. It was blood stained.

"Am I going to die? My stomach hurts something awful. I don't want to die!" she screamed. Behind a screen Louise examined her.

"Kate!" Louise called out after a few moments. "I want you to get me a cup of strong hot tea and don't fill it all the way to the top." Kate returned with a steaming mug, curious to know what kind of emergency required tea.

"So, you're telling me this started during exercises?" Louise addressed the girl as she rummaged through a cupboard. She pulled out a small bottle of 'India Brandy' and poured a good amount into the tea. She handed it to her patient. The girl nodded. "I've split meself haven't I?"

"No, you haven't split yourself," said Louise stifling a laugh, "and you're not going to die. Drink the brandy it'll help with the cramps. How old are you?"

At the taste of the doctored tea the girl's face distorted as though she'd sucked lemons. "Twelve."

"Hasn't anyone talked to you about…what happens to girls each month?" The girl shook her head.

"Heavens!" said Louise.

"It's the curse," Kate whispered to the girl, whose face registered an understanding of the phrase.

Louise addressed her question to Kate. "Do the sisters keep supplies for…" Kate shook her head. "I don't know."

"Then how do you manage?" said Louise.

Kate was reluctant to say.

"Answer me! I can't help if you don't tell me."

"We cut up towels, make holes in each end and use string to hold it on," said Kate and looked at the floor.

"Good Lord!" said Louise.

Louise confronted the sisters that same day.

"There's a part of the girls education that appears to be lacking." She explained the case she'd had earlier in the day. "The poor girl was terrified."

"It's not something one talks about...its unclean!" said Sister Constance.

"I've been taking care of the boys," said Sister Theresa. "I've got my hands full with problems there but I suppose I could..."

"I want to see all the girls, from the age of nine on up, at three o' clock this afternoon. Supplies will be acquisitioned from the dispensary," Louise said.

"It never occurred to me," she continued, after the nuns had left. "Kate is there anything else I don't know about?"

"Well, we could use some waterproof sheets," said Kate without hesitation.

"What?"

"Some of the girls started wetting their beds at night right after they came on the ship. It's hard to get the mattresses dry."

"Where in the world am I to get waterproof sheets?"

Kate shrugged her shoulders.

"Anything else?"

"Mice!" said Kate. "We need to do something about the mice."

Every evening John and Louise strolled around the deck and talked. Louise told him all about Kate. "She's strong, like I had to be, and I see a lot of myself in her. We've become good friends," said Louise. "She's had such a rough time of things, John. She's so determined to go back to England and find her brother. Her mother may not be alive...tuberculosis, I think. It was never personal before, John, but now it is. I only ever saw the names and numbers on pieces of paper."

"It's like war," said John trying to keep the wind from blowing out the match as he lit a cigarette. "Noble and glamorized, in the newspapers, but until you're knee deep in muck and doing things that go against principle does it dawn on you what reality is. What happens to them all when we get there?"

"A few of the children are being met at the dock by prospective families. I've decided that Kate will stay with me. I'll sign the papers for

64

guardian-ship. The others will go by train to trade schools and then be farmed out. Mentally and physically it's been so hard on them." After a long silence Louise said, "I don't suppose you'd know where there's any waterproof material on board?"

"That's the second time I've been asked that question," said John.

"Who?"

"Sister Theresa. She and the Sergeant almost got into a knock down drag out fight when he caught her trying to steal a couple of tents."

"Tents?"

"Seems a few of the boys have a bed-wetting problem; 'stress' she said. Needed waterproof sheets. Sergeant wouldn't let her have them so she tried to pinch 'em."

Louise laughed. "Wish I'd have been there to see that. Some of the girls are having the same problem. So now what do we do? "

"It just… so… happens," said John, "that the lifeboats are covered by…"

Louise laughed out loud. "What would I do without you, John Reynolds?"

"If you play your cards right you won't have to." His tone was serious

"Play my cards right?"

"You could marry me."

They stood at the rail of the ship facing each other. John's eyes were serious and intent.

There was a long silence while Louise studied his face.

"Now why do you suppose I would want to do that?" she asked, her tone teasing but with an undercurrent of seriousness.

"Because you love me." John put his arms around her waist and pulled her close.

"You're very sure of yourself!" Louise said.

"Oh, yes… very sure."

"Well, you could have picked a better time to ask me. Look at me…my hair' frizzed out like a Picannini's and… "

"I am looking." John looked at her unruly hair and the worn cable-knit cardigan she'd borrowed from one of the crew, after the last child had thrown up on her. He looked at her fresh complexion and at her soft brown eyes and thought about how beautiful she was. He tilted her chin up and kissed her. Louise pulled away with a sudden thought. "But what about Kate?" John laughed and said, "She'll love Willoughby!"

The second case to be brought to the dispensary was a fourteen-year old boy called Colin Smith. He had chills yet his skin was hot and sticky from sweat. He suffered delirium and a deep croup-like cough. The whites of his eyes were pink from fever. Doctor Porter listened to his chest and back, with the stethoscope, then drew his eyebrows together when he heard the tight wheezing congestion in the lungs.

"I can hear it from hear. Its pneumonia isn't it?" said Louise.

"Afraid so. He'll need watching round the clock. Needs to breathe steam. I'll get the Sergeant to get a couple of the men to see about getting some kettles of water up here, coals from the boiler room and we'll need to make a tent to keep the steam in. Not much else we can do way out here miles from anywhere!"

Louise sat by the boy night after night. Jack Porter came in about two in the morning. He had a mug of tea in his hand.

"My shift," he said. "Thought you could use a cup of tea. How's he doing?" Louise shook her head. "No change." Porter sat sideways on the bed and ran his hand across the boy's brow. "I've got a son about his age, you know?"

"No, I didn't know," said Louise.

"Why aren't you at home raising a family of your own, pretty girl like you?"

"It's a long story," said Louise.

"And what's the story with you and that Reynolds chap? Is it serious?"

"Yes, he's asked me to marry him," said Louise but there was no joy in her reply. All she could think about was the sick child and a strong responsibility for him being there. She expressed this to Jack Porter.

"That's ridiculous. Probably some street urchin living from hand to mouth in the gutters. What chance would he have had back there? He has food, clothing and people who care enough about him to see that he knows how to take care of himself. "They aren't all street urchins," said Louise. "It's just that I'm beginning to see two sides to this."

After three days the fever hadn't broken. Porter, Louise and Kate had taken shifts watching the boy. Sister Theresa came often and sat next to him and counted each Hail Mary on her rosary beads.

"Colin is a good boy," she said to Louise, tearfully. "Never a bit of trouble. Always up on deck talking to the soldiers. Wanted to know where they were going and where they'd been. It's things like this that shake your faith in God."

Louise took Sister Theresa's arm. "Come on Sister, let's walk on the deck a while shall we? Kate, keep an eye on Colin for me and come and get me if anything changes, will you?"

Kate sat alone and watched the boy. He struggled for every breath. She wrung out a cloth in cool water and wiped his forehead. She studied Colin's face with its high cheekbones and thin nose. He made her think of Harry. What would Harry look like when he was fourteen. Would she even know him? Colin's eyelashes fluttered and Kate heard the rattles in the boy's throat. His chest heaved and then became still. Although Kate had never seen death before…she knew. "*Mrs. Wilson!*" she screamed and ran for the door

On the upper deck, the entire ship gathered in somber silence as a canvas stretcher was brought to the rail of the deck. A khaki army blanket covered the form of the young man who had dreamed of becoming a soldier. The children were wide-eyed and stood a little closer to each other. The soldiers stood in formation with chins high in the air. The crew had their hands clasped in front of them. John reached for Louise's hand while the nuns said prayers. Louise put her hand to her throat when the stretcher was tilted and the occupant disappeared from under the blanket. A splash was heard and it was over. The nuns crossed themselves then stood in a moment of silence before clapping their hands to dismiss the children.

CHAPTER TEN
Collections and Returns

The children, tired from the voyage were led to a rail yard where they waited for the train. Two boys and two girls had been singled out to meet with their benefactors. They'd been chosen for various reasons…farm labourers, domestics or companions. They were escorted to the station's pavilion by Sister Theresa. A big man in blue overalls walked over to one of the boys and said gruffly, "What's yer name lad and how old would yer be?"

"Alfred, I'm fourteen."

"Kinda wiry. Let me see yer 'ands." After looking at the boy's hands the man felt his arms. "You look fit enough and you're no stranger to work judging by those calluses. I can promise you a roof over yer 'ead and you'll be fed, but I'll expect you to work 'ard. I don't tolerate laziness, so we'll get that straight for a start. This one'll do and I'll take the other one too. Where do I sign for them, Sister? My 'Missus' and me need to get started back."

Alfred was left behind with the 'Missus'. Her grey hair was knotted into a bun at the nape of her neck. A black handbag, that was too large, dangled from the crook of her arm and her brown coat barely stretched to meet the buttons. Black lace- up shoes had heels worn down, on the outside, giving the woman a slight bow-legged look. She stood in front of Alfred and smiled at him. He looked at her with suspicion.

"Don't pay any mind to him, he talks rough but he's soft as pudding. He'll treat yer fair. Now then, tell me, do you like to eat?" Alfred nodded with great vigor.

"Well, we're already off to a good start then aren't we? I like to cook. I make the best suet dumplings you ever tasted." She put her arm around Alfred's shoulder.

"It'll be nice having someone around who appreciates my cooking!" She didn't tell Alfred that her boy had been lost in the war.

An elegantly dressed couple zeroed in on a rosy cheeked blond haired little girl who was about seven. The woman wore a black suit with a matching cloche hat with the front brim turned up. Like Mary Pickford and Clara Bow her lips were thin and perfectly penciled to a bright red cupid's bow. She raised her over-plucked eyebrows and addressed her husband.

"Oh! she's exactly what we were looking for, isn't she Harold," the woman said, her voice loud and gushing with falseness in the airs and graces she did not possess. She turned to one of the nuns.

"She'll be a sister for our daughter, Beryl. I do trust the girl doesn't have any bad habits?" she whispered to the Sister from behind her gloved hand.

"We have a housekeeper, you know, don't we Harold." The long suffering Harold, impotent in the presence of his wife, nodded his head in agreement.

"Can she sew," asked a plain faced woman with eagerness, "and can she cook? How is she with taking care of children and cleaning?"

"Agnes is fifteen and has been trained to do all of those things. She'll get a small stipend from you, sort of pocket money, for savings."

"I've got six children at home, the oldest is eight. I need the help. Now, you say if we adopt her we don't have to pay her anything, is that right?"

"Yes, that's right." Sister Theresa looked uneasy. Agnes was crestfallen when she heard what was expected of her.

"Do I have to go sister? Can't I say no?"

"It'll be alright, child, The Agency will check on you and if you're not happy with the situation then you'll be placed in another home."

"What about school. Will I be able to go to school?"

"There's no school where we live," said the woman.

A girl about seven stood with her arms folded. The couple looked at the little girl with her scraped up knees and bony frame. Her hair was mousy brown and stuck out in every direction. She patted her hair self-consciously. The girl had brown eyes, the colour of dried mud, and not too many places on her face had escaped freckles. She was the most startling child Bill and Edna Jenkins had ever seen. The girl smiled at the couple, displaying missing upper front teeth.

"I'm getting my big girl teeth," the child chirped by way of explanation.

"There must be some mistake," Edna said to Sister Theresa. "We wrote asking for…"

"You don't want me do you?" said the girl. She was direct. "You want someone pretty and I'm plain."

"It's not that at all," said Edna. "We'd asked for someone much… younger."

"They said I was too plain and wouln'tcha know it… now I'm too old!"

Bill Jenkins could barely hide the amusement he felt listening to this child. "Who said you were too plain?"

"Back at the school, the others said I was."

"What's your name?" said Bill Jenkins.

The girl hesitated for a moment then said, "Violet. What's yours?"

Shy Violet', thought Bill Jenkins. Someone had a sense of humour but he suspected Violet had heard it all before, judging by her hesitation in answering.

"I like her…she's quite a character," Bill said.

"I know you do, she's outspoken, just like you," said Edna. She plucked at her husband's sleeve to caution him.

"Well, my wife and I will have to discuss this first, Violet. Maybe we can sit and visit awhile, get to know you a little better before we decide. Edna Jenkins knew the decision had already been made and hoped Violet would like the pink bedroom that was waiting for her.

John was watching the scene as he and Kate waited for Louise and he wondered what his boy must have felt as someone chose him for one reason or another.

"There you are," said Louise and kissed John on the cheek.

"So where do we go from here," John asked.

"Well, the town of Mundy isn't on the map. The nearest place is McGregor. I have the directions." John took the map from Louise. "Lot of places out here aren't recorded."

The train whistle blew. "That's us!" Louise said and picked up a suitcase.

CHAPTER ELEVEN
McGregor

The town of McGregor looked affluent. John drove past the bank, church and shops and parked outside the Wallace Hotel.

"Get us a couple of rooms, Louise, while I see what I can find out." John slammed the car door and looked up and down the street.

"What are you looking for?" Louise asked.

"Somewhere sheep drovers go to. They travel around and would be more likely to know what's going on at the surrounding stations. I'll meet you and Kate back here later."

Further up the street John found a place with horses tethered outside. *'Last Stand,'* it said over the door. John reached for the brass doorknob. It was loose and tarnished with age. As John's eyes adjusted from the bright outdoors to the interior of the place he saw a well-polished wooden bar on the right of the room and shelves of tinned and dry goods behind a counter on the left. In the center of the room a few miss-matched chairs and tables were scattered about. A woman was helping a sheep drover fill a canvas bag with sacks of salt, flour and other supplies. Several drovers stood at the bar drinking tea of all things. They were laughing at some tall story one of them had told. Two old men sat across from each other playing dominoes.

"What can I do for you?" the barkeep asked. He was a short, balding man with the hint of a Scottish accent.

"Beer," said Reynolds. The barkeep pulled a handle directing the beer to the side of the glass to prevent the suds from spilling over. It rose and spilled anyway.

"Just passing through," said John.

"Where are you from?" asked the barkeep.

"Willoughby."

"I've heard of it." The barkeep had noticed the scar on John's temple and the very slight limp when he walked in. "War?" he asked.

"A long time ago."

"So what brings you to McGregor?" A fly, attracted to the spilled beer was swatted with a wet cotton rag.

"I'm looking for a man named Patrick Riley. I don't have an address, just a town called Mundy. It's not on the map."

"What do you want with him? You a friend of his?" said the barkeep, the welcoming smile leaving his face and his body stiffening. Reynolds could tell from the man's reaction that a wall had gone up. Since he needed the information quickly he decided to lay all his cards on the table.

"No. Never met him. I think he has my son. My boy was sent from England...as a migrant. It was a mistake. I was away in France...didn't find out until now."

"I know who Riley is," said the barkeep. His voice relayed a tone that revealed knowing Patrick Riley was not a pleasant experience. "We get a lot of migrant children coming here. They do alright. Don't recall hearing about Riley having a boy out there. Wouldn't want any kin of mine living with the likes of him."

"Why?"

"He's a bully, likes to pick fights when he's had a few. Intimidates my customers into paying for his drinks...what we call *'a man with deep pockets and short arms.'* Tight with his money if you know what I mean. Wife died a few years ago. He's got money but nobody knows where he gets it from. Never worked a day in his life has that one. Daughter lives with him, Mary. Don't know how she puts up with him."

"Where does he live?"

"Next town over or what's left of it. Used to be called Mundy but now it's all part of McGregor." The barkeep put down the cloth and stood on the balls of his feet to call out over the drone of conversation in the room.

"Anyone know anything about a boy up at Riley's place?" No-one spoke.

"C'mon you lot, this bloke is one of ours...back from the war. It's his boy he's looking for."

One of the old men, playing dominoes, scraped his chair across the floor as he pushed back away from the table. Reynolds assessed the man to be in his seventies. His hair was white and a bushy moustache, yellowed from tobacco, drooped like the whiskers of a walrus. He reached for a cane that hung on the back of his chair. A black and white border collie came out from under the table and followed him, nose against the man's heel. The old man had a prominent disability that forced him to lean heavily on his cane as he gyrated in a rolling gait towards Reynolds.

"Never seen the boy, myself," the man said.

"Sam runs the local newspaper," said the barkeep. "He knows everything that goes on here."

"Well, I wouldn't go so far as to say that, but a year back I did hear someone claim Riley had tried to sell him a boy. Farm labourers are in high demand out here."

"Sell?" said John.

"With the influx of migrant children into the country it's not the first time that's happened. Most are taken in by good people but there are the odd ones who don't care to ask where their help comes from. In my 'pinion it's not a good idea sending those children here...pale skin can't take the sun, for a start."

"Didn't someone report Riley or even go out there?" John asked.

"We did. Went with the constable myself. He searched every inch of Riley's place but didn't find anything. Nobody out there but Riley and his daughter. No evidence he ever had a boy out there."

"I have a woman with me who can prove Riley signed for this boy."

"You're sure about this?"

"Yes!"

Sam looked thoughtful for a moment. "If he's in the buying and selling business you realize Riley probably got rid of the boy a long time ago? In my 'pinion..."

"I don't really want to hear your opinion! Just tell me how I can find the bastard!" John's raised voice caused the black and white collie to rumble in the back of his throat and move in front of Sam. The fur stood up in a ridge down his back and his tail was raised. Sam snapped his fingers at the dog and it lay down. "Riley is a nasty piece of work, I can tell you. You'll need the constable to go with you."

Having left Kate back at the Wallace Hotel, John and Louise drove out in the direction of Mundy. Earlier Constable Oxley had told them, "Suit yourselves but I don't think you should go out there, just the two of you. If you'll just wait until tomorrow I'll be able to go with you."

"I've waited too long already," John said. Reluctantly the Constable had given John directions on how to find the Riley place.

"Shouldn't be hard to find a boy fitting that description," Oxley said. "Red hair, birthmark… and Declan, well… that's not a name I've ever heard of before, 'course the name could have been changed. With the papers, you brought, Riley can't wriggle out of the fact that he had the boy. He'll have to produce him. Riley's daughter's name's Mary. She'll know if the boy's been there, if you can get her to talk to you."

John leaned forward when they reached the dilapidated old town of Mundy. It looked like a stripped carcass. It had bloomed, in its day, faded and shriveled into its last years of life, waiting only for that final gust of wind to blow what was left of it away.

A little further out, the Riley place came into view. Isolated and run down, the single story dwelling had a corrugated tin roof as did the three sheds that sat in back of it. At the right of the main house a lone dead tree, bleached by the sun, spread skeletal fingers of branches that seemed to point downward to the small figure of a girl laboriously scrubbing clothes over a washboard. The girl looked up and shaded her eyes to see who was coming.

John and Louise walked towards her and from a distance could see that she'd pulled the back of her skirt up, between her knees, and tucked it into the front waistband to keep the hem out of the spilled water. As they got closer they were shocked to see her condition. She had dried blood caked in her hair and an ugly bruise across her left cheek. Her legs were covered in red welts and her bottom lip was badly swollen. She wore no shoes.

"*Jesus!*" said John. Louise moved forward and the girl backed away from her.

"It's alright," said Louise. "Are you Mary? We're looking for a boy. He's about seven years old. Declan Thomas. Is he here?" Mary, her eyes full of terror glanced towards the house.

"Leave. You shouldn't be here."

"Where's your father?"

The girl's eyes darted again towards the house. "I said leave…there'll be trouble." Her hair was matted and unkempt and knuckles raw from being rubbed against the corrugated washboard. Her shoulders slouched.

"Your father did this to you?" said Louise. John was already striding towards the front door, his fists clenched.

"Don't!" Mary shouted after him. "You'll make it worse!" Mary tried to stop John as he entered the house but Louise held her back. The three roomed house was clean and scrubbed but there was no sign of any luxury in the sparsely furnished place and no sign of Riley. Louise had dipped a cloth in the water bucket and dabbed at the girls face. "Your own Father …how could he…"

"He's not my father!" shouted the girl and pulled herself away from Louise.

"Then who are you?"

After some hesitation she said, "Mary Sellers. I looked after the Missus until she died."

"How did you get here?" asked Louise.

"On the boat, like the others."

"Good God!" said Louise.

"You said others. Are there others…here?" John had come out of the house and overheard the conversation. His attentions were on the girl.
They didn't see Riley come from behind the house. Before John could hear the answer to his question Riley had swung a sturdy tree branch at John's head, felling him to his knees and knocking him unconscious.

"Don't you say another word to them girl or you'll get the back of my hand across you, now come towards me," Riley shouted and lunged at the girl.

Somewhere in his sixties, Riley was heavyset with several days' growth of stubble on his face. He was quick for such a heavy man. He wore a white tank top stained yellow with sweat. Khaki coloured trousers hung under his paunched stomach. Suspenders, still attached, hung down over his hips in two loops. Mary crouched instinctively and covered her head with her arms but Riley grabbed her wrist and yanked her towards him.

"Trespassing! That's what you people are doing…now get off my place!" Riley's eyes bulged and his face twisted with anger. He waved the branch to keep distance between himself, Louise and John while he gripped Mary's wrist.

"Constable Oxley's on his way out here and has a warrant for your arrest!" said Louise.

"Is that so?"

"Mary… you signed for her and there were others." Louise had been edging away from John, turning Riley in her direction. She'd spotted something Riley hadn't…John was regaining consciousness.

"Mary is mine fair and square, I've got papers to prove it. Is that what this is all about?"

"Oh, no Mr. Riley! It's much more than that. There's a boy missing. You signed for him. I want to know where he is and I'll be checking to see how many others you signed for. It's about selling children Mr. Riley! Isn't that what you've been doing here?" John had gotten to his feet and threw himself at Riley. He choked him in the crook of his arm until he got him to the ground. Riley elbowed Reynolds in the ribs to get him away from him. John hauled off and aimed a punch at Riley's jaw. Riley sprawled on his back and then sat up. He spat blood onto the sand.

"You'll be sorry you did that!" he said. Blows were exchanged until Reynolds got Riley down and straddled him. Except for Riley's face, everything around John seemed to disappear in a grey fog. Somewhere outside the fog he could hear Louise's voice telling him to stop but he continued to pummel Riley's face with his fists. He couldn't stop…he didn't want to. Years of anger from the war and the loss of Maggie went into every blow. The punches got slower as John tired. His chest heaved as he tried to catch his breath.

"You'll kill him!" Louise screamed. "What good will that do?" The greyness cleared and John rolled away from Riley. He staggered over to the washtub and dipped his head in it then dunked the bucket and went to Riley and dumped the water over his face. Riley stirred and groaned.

"Tell me where my boy is or I'll finish the job!" said John his voice barely a gasp.

"I'll tell you," Mary said then covered her mouth with her hands.

"You shut your mouth girl!" Riley said as he pointed at her. John yanked one of the suspenders from Riley's trousers and tied his hands behind him. Mary, seeing she was in no more danger said, "He's under that first shed." She pointed to one of the outbuildings. "There's a cellar under the floor." John was already running.

"He's been down there two days," said Mary to Louise. John reached the shed. The planks of wood were curled from dryness and weather, sun-bleached grey and rotted. Sheep had cribbed and chewed at it and John could hear the loud drone of flies inside. As John entered the shed the stench made him reel. He put his arm over his nose and mouth and searched for the opening to the cellar. There it was…a metal ring in the floor. He pulled and flung the door up and over. It crashed onto the floor. John climbed down into the darkness below. He waited for his eyes to adjust. The room was little more than a dug out and a few degrees cooler. In the corner he saw something…a small shape that didn't move. A cry escaped John when he saw the small figure lying in the corner. He turned the child over and placed his two fingers against the throat…there was a pulse…faint but nonetheless a pulse. John lifted the boy up and climbed back out of the pit. He ran with the limp child in his arms.

In the daylight he could see the thin emaciated boy, encrusted with dirt on his blistered skin, with sores, insect bites, dry cracked lips and bruises.

"Get some water that's fit to drink," said John and took the boy into the house and laid him on the table. "Louise for God's sake help me! Do something for him!" John stood aside as Louise went to work to assess the situation. "He's barely alive. We'll have to get him to McGregor. Get him in the car."

"You're not going to leave me here are you?" Mary cried out. She wrung her hands together, her eyes wide with terror. "He'll kill me. He did terrible things to me. It wasn't my fault."

"I should have finished the job!" said John and headed for the door.

"No!" said Louise and grabbed his sleeve. "There's no time! We have to get the boy to McGregor as soon as we can. Mary get in the car." John picked up the boy and carried him outside. He laid him across the back seat with his head resting in Mary's lap.

"You wouldn't dare leave me out here tied up!" shouted Riley. The car roared into action leaving a trail of dust behind as it headed for McGregor.

Doctor Evens was out on a call so the local vet was the next best thing.

"Never seen anything like it. Look how badly his feet are festered. He's dehydrated, emaciated and he's taken quite a beating."

Constable Oxley kept his composure but the anger was evident in the muscles that twitched in his jaw when he saw the condition of the boy.

"I'll go bring Riley in," he said. "He'll be lucky if a lynch-mob doesn't string him up before he gets to court and I'm not so sure I'd want to stop them."

"You ought to put him in the same hole he put the boy. Padlock it and leave him there to die. That would be justice!" said Louise.

"Is he your boy?" asked the Constable.

John looked at the small figure on the table. Layers of filth hid hair and skin colouring. "I think so."

"Mary said the boy hadn't been with Riley all that long. Didn't come out from England until he was six. Every time Riley sold him he ran and was hauled back and put in the cellar. That didn't set too well with Riley as he'd spent the money. We all thought Mary was his daughter. His wife got sickly and died a while back."

"He forced himself on Mary," said Louise. "That poor girl…"

"She told us," said Constable Oxley. "That was why the boy got the beating. He tried to stop Riley from hurting her. Riley had quite a trade going there. Farm labor for sale, been four children passed through his place, that we know of."

"I don't know how they stayed alive," said Louise.

"Mary was so hungry," said Constable Oxley, "but when my wife put a plate of meat and potatoes in front of her she just sat there looking at it and cried. Said she'd eaten food that was infested with maggots. If we'd have known what was going on out there…"

"The law won't do much to him," said the vet.

"If what Mary says is right, there's one buried out there," said Constable Oxley. The room fell silent.

"How could that have happened?" said Louise. "How could anyone not know what was going on out there?"

"Riley's place is a fair distance from here. All we had were rumours… never any proof of anyone else out there and, believe me, I looked."

"But didn't you talk to Mary?"

"She wouldn't open her mouth with him around. Thought he was her daughter, we all did." Louise put her hand to her throat and her eyes filled with tears.

The Vet cleared his throat. "Mrs. Wilson?"

Louise didn't respond. Her eyes were fixed on Constable Oxley. "Mrs. Wilson, I could use a hand here."

"Yes," she said and wiped her eyes with the back of her hand. "I'll get him washed and cleaned up right away."

"Got to get some fluids into him first," said the vet. That same evening the boy lay in a clean bed. He still wasn't conscious. Louise let John into the room and closed the door quietly.

"It's him," John whispered. "It's my son." The dark carrot red hair was unmistakable. The features were hard to tell because of bruising and swelling.

"There's a small birthmark on the back of his neck," said Louise. "He's your son, John. Mary never knew his name. Riley just called him, 'Boy'.

John closed his eyes. His feelings were mixed…relief, anger, sadness, joy.

"He will be alright, won't he Louise?" he asked..

"Yes. He won't be able to travel for a few weeks but he's going to be fine."

"I'll need to send a telegram to his mother, tomorrow, let her know he's been found."

"I'll go with you," said Louise. "I need to contact The Agency about all this."

The next two weeks the good people of McGregor rallied to the needs of their guests. There hospitality was overwhelming to Louise. She was touched by the kindness and thought about how difficult it would be to leave this town and these people.

Sam's newspaper carried a full front page article about the deplorable condition the children had been found. The article made the London papers. It also mentioned that Patrick Riley had not been found. Constable Oxley had been out to Mundy but claimed he never found Riley.

"Probably ran off or fell down a hole somewhere on his property," he'd said. He certainly was making no effort to look for Riley. Constable Oxley didn't feel the need. He thought Louise Wilson to be a very clever woman.

"The boy doesn't talk," said Doctor Evans. "Probably shock. He'll be fit enough to travel by the end of the week though."

"We've got a good Doctor in Willoughby who'll take care of him," said John.

"What will happen to Mary? Will she be sent back to England?" said Evans.

"No. Louise and I thought we'd take her to Willoughby with us. A friend of mine has an hotel there. She's offered Mary a job and clean room plus we'll be close by to keep an eye on things. She'll be well looked after," said John.

"That's good to know," Evans said.

James Mannington always read the London newspapers. He read the article about Declan Thomas and Mary Sellers twice.

"Thomas!" he shouted at the top of his lungs, "I want to send a telegram and I want to see Phoebe...*now*! Do you hear me? Thomas, where in the hell are you?"

"Is everything alright sir?" asked Thomas coming at a run.

"It will be. Help me get dressed; I have to go out!"

"Out sir?"

CHAPTER TWELVE
Preparations

It had always been referred to as 'the big bedroom'. The handsome oak furniture consisted of a large bed with high rounded headboard, a bow fronted wardrobe, triple mirrored dressing table with stool and a tallboy chest of drawers. The room caught the morning sun through double windows. French doors opened out onto the veranda.

"I'm putting John and Louise in my old room. Well, the truth of it is I just thought it would be easier for them not to be in the same room John and Maggie shared," said Mum. Sadie agreed. Mum gave Sadie a quick glance and continued. "We can fix it up, bit of white paint and wallpaper, it shouldn't take us long." Mum turned her attention to the white lace curtains. Sadie put her hands on her hips, angled her head, and gave Mum a knowing look.

"What do you mean…we? 'Help me move a few bits of furniture, give everything a good polish and we'll have tea,' you said. There was no mention of wallpapering!"

"You promised to help me. We've only got three days before they get here," said Mum.

"But the walls have to be stripped and I'll have to mix buckets of flour paste." Sensing victory Mum said, "I sent away for the wallpaper last month. It's under the bed." Sadie rolled her eyes towards the ceiling then got down on her knees and felt around under the bed. Several rolls of paper emerged. Mum opened one of them displaying pale peach roses on a white background. She held it out to Sadie. "What do you think?"

"I think you got me out here under false pretenses," said Sadie and groaned.

"I'll go and put the kettle on for a cup of tea while you get started," said Mum and disappeared through the doorway.

"Better be cake with that tea old woman!" Sadie shouted after her and gave an exaggerated sigh as she started taking the curtains down. Mum smiled to herself as she walked to the kitchen. She was a woman who got things done.

"I never realized Australia was so green," Kate said as she looked out of the car window.

John wasn't listening. He was studying Louise's pensive expression. The closer they got to Willoughby the more uncertain she became. Louise wondered if John's friends and family would be able to accept her? How could they when they loved Maggie so much.

"Getting cold feet?" said John and patted her hand. Louise nodded. Declan obeyed instructions but still hadn't spoken. Mary just looked out the window of the train, arms folded, legs crossed...silent. She wondered what was going to happen to her and what lay ahead of her *this* time. Kate was talkative, interested in everything she saw.

As soon as the car stopped in front of the house, Mum was out in the driveway. She'd heard the car coming and could barely contain her excitement. "They're here, Sadie!" she shouted back to the house. Mum jiggled Alice on her hip more from nervousness than to soothe the child.

The screen-door squeaked as Sadie came outside. All Louise's fears dissipated as Mum and Sadie surrounded her with hugs and chatter. "What a long trip you've had, dear, you must be exhausted. Not to worry though, got a nice pot of tea on the hob and there's pie," said Mum. Without ceremony she handed Alice to John and kissed him on the cheek.

John looked at his daughter then tousled her hair. "Well Miss Alice Reynolds," he said. "We've got a lot of making up to do." Alice screamed bloody murder and tried to get out of this stranger's grasp. Everyone was hustled up the steps and into the house. All except Declan. Mum had watched the boy, for a moment, as she greeted Louise. The look in his eyes reminded her of a half-starved injured Dingo she and Dad had found in one of the sheds one year. It had wanted the food she held out to it, but held back...not trusting her intentions. Mum knew that Declan wasn't approachable...at least not yet. Without looking at the boy she called over her shoulder, "It's apple pie. You look like a lad who could do it justice. Come in when you're ready." The screen door smacked shut behind her.

After tea John went to unpack the car.

"Sadie, why don't you show Louise her new home while I see about Alice," said Mum. Sadie led the way upstairs. "Better show you your room first. John's is down on the first floor…just 'til the wedding. You know how it is." Louise entered the bedroom and stood beside Sadie.

"It's beautiful!" Louise said. She touched the peach bedspread and admired the lace curtains that gently billowed into the room.

"Glad you think so," said Sadie and smiled. The conversation was a little stiff and forced, small talk about the weather and the Blackburn Hotel.

"You own the hotel?" said Louise. She already knew this from John but decided it might be a topic of conversation.

"I do," said Sadie. "It's a lot of work I can tell you. With the train bringing so many people in its constantly busy. It's hard to find good help. Mary will be a Godsend I can tell you. Maggie was always onto me to…" Sadie stopped abruptly when she realized she'd said Maggie's name. She slapped the front of her forehead with the palm of her hand. "Stupid woman I am. I didn't mean to…"

Louise smiled. "Sadie, cards on the table. Hearing Maggie's name doesn't bother me. Not hearing it would put barriers between us. Tell me about Maggie. What was she like?"

"I grew up with her. She was like a sister to me. Sweetest natured person I ever met. Positive about everything. It hurt Mum to see John give in to the grief. He couldn't deal with losing Maggie. He had us all worried. I'll help you all I can, Louise."

"May I ask you something?" Louise said.

"Look, love, "I know what you're going to ask. Yes, we loved Maggie dearly but she's gone. You're what John needs now and you'll be accepted just as she was. You'll fit in here, I promise."

"No, it's not that," said Louise, "I wanted to ask…"

"If this was Maggie's room? No, love, it wasn't."

"I was going to ask where the toilet is?" Both women stood in silence then burst out laughing.

"You and I are going to get along just fine… once we learn to communicate," said Sadie.

"What are you two finding so funny?" John asked as he came through the door carrying two suitcases. Louise smiled at him. "I'm going to like it here John," she said.

CHAPTER THIRTEEN
Settling In

"It's so exciting! Willoughby hasn't had a church wedding in years," Sadie said.

"The whole town's coming. White dress, flowers...I've planned everything."

"But I thought it would be just..." began Louise.

"Oh, it's going to be wonderful," said Sadie with exaggerated enthusiasm. "The reception's at the hotel...it's all arranged!"

"I can't, not in a church, not in a white dress. You don't understand... I was married before," said Louise.

"I know," Sadie said her voice full of sympathy. "But this isn't England Louise. You can do anything you please. This is a place for new beginnings and second chances. That's what Australia is all about."

"I thought John and I would be marrying in a registry office. Even if I agreed to get married in the church I have nothing to wear."

"But you do... my dress. Like your husband, my fiancé didn't make it back either. I still have the dress. We look to be about the same size, Louise."

"I'm... sorry about your fiancé. Look, I couldn't possibly..." Louise began. Sadie silenced her. "Yes you can. Since it looks like I'm to be an old maid I'd at least like to see my dress going down the aisle, even if I'm not the one wearing it." The two women linked arms and headed for the car.

The bans were read, announcing the upcoming wedding, for three consecutive weeks at the church. Preparations for the event had the whole town full of anticipation.

Mary proved to be adept at waiting tables at the Blackburn Hotel. The work was easy, the people friendly and she was delighted with her room.

Kate and Mum had formed a close alliance but Kate still had her sights set on returning to England to find Harry.

John wondered what Declan thought about him as a father. The boy still hadn't spoken but Dr. Phillips said he would speak 'in his own good time'. Declan had retreated behind an expressionless face, his emotions unreadable. Mum's description of her grandson had been 'an old head on young shoulders'. Declan was quick to learn. He took to riding the broad-backed stock horses like a natural. He had an ease with horses and the dogs that he didn't have with people.

Eventually John would teach him everything about running the station since one day it would be Declan's. Into the third week John observed the boy's eyes light up with interest when the shearers took the fleece off the sheep in one piece. He seemed fascinated by the competition between the men as they laughed about who was the fastest at shearing. He helped get the wool baled up, ready to take to the train, but didn't join the men when they ate the huge plates of cold mutton, beans and bread the women fixed. Instead he preferred to hang back, be on the perimeter of things, an observer. His only interaction was with Alice. There seemed to be a silent communication between the two. Alice's eyes followed her brother everywhere. Declan anticipated her needs, whether it was to pass a toy that was out of her reach or remove a dangerous object from her path. Alice smiled and burbled unintelligible words to him.

There was one small chink in the barrier Declan had set up around himself. It surfaced the day Mum was mixing a cake for Sunday tea. Declan sat and watched her scrape the mixture into a pan when John came in.

"Can I lick the bowl?" he said and winked at Declan.

"No you can't!" said Mum. "You'll flush the toilet like everyone else!" Declan almost laughed. Mum's eyes made contact with John's. It was the first sign something was changing. Mum talked to Declan about England and about his grandfather and about John when he was a little boy. She showed him photographs and told him about the tragedy of Maggie and how Alice was born with no mother. "But you carry on and make a life for yourself lad, just like I did and your Dad and Louise and even little Alice."

John was at the barbershop getting a haircut four days before the wedding when Sadie put her head round the door and called to him. "You've got a visitor John. He's at the hotel. Looks pretty important. Says he wants to see you." John looked confused.

"James Mannington, from England. Came in on the train. He's in a wheelchair, said you'd know who he was. Good looking bloke." John sat for a moment and frowned then stood up, took the towel from his neck, and followed Sadie.

James Mannington tapped his fingers nervously on the arms of the wheelchair as he waited in the carpeted lobby of the hotel. The journey had been long but not unpleasant. It was good to be out in the world again. James had been angry for so long about his disability. It wasn't something he could accept. He hated being dependent, hated it. He'd been so active and involved in everything...before. When James returned from the war it didn't occur to him that the affliction would be permanent even though the doctors had said it would be. He always believed he'd get the use of his legs back. Nothing really sank in until months later. His moods eliminated friends when he shrank from any social contact. All he could see, thought James, was what he couldn't do, what he couldn't have.

The catalyst for his anger had been Phoebe's pregnancy. What a waste his life had been. John walked towards James then stopped. He said nothing.

"Hello, John. Surprised to see me? I didn't think you'd answer if I wrote or sent a telegram so I came instead. Took a chance that if I came all this way you wouldn't refuse to see me."

John put his hands in his pockets, not knowing what to say.

"I read the story about the boy in the London papers," James continued. "I know how you must hate me for what I did but I came here to tell you I was wrong. I did have the telegram sent to you giving the location of the boy. I assume that's what led to him being found?"

John ran his fingers through his hair.

"You're not going to make this easy for me are you?" said James. "You and I need to think about what's best for the boy. It's not about us anymore, John. He'll need good schools. I won't be around forever. One day Baden Hall will be his. We'll need to prepare him for that. I thought perhaps you'd agree to him coming to England for school; the summers he'd spend with you."

"I didn't know it was you who had the telegram sent," said John. "He's had a rough time of it. The boy isn't ready to go anywhere just yet, James. He's still recovering. He hasn't spoken a word, but you can see him." John's voice held no hostility.

"John, this was a difficult journey for me. I had plenty of time to think. I have much to account for, but I want you to know I'm trying to make amends. I have a job at The Agency, now. The program is basically a good one but the system needs revision to make sure something like this doesn't happen again. Give me another chance, John." Reynolds stepped behind the wheelchair and pushed. "We've all been part of what's happened, James. What do you say we talk about it…over a beer?"

"I'd like that," said James.

"Can't believe you came all this way by yourself," said John.

"Oh, I didn't. Thomas came with me." John stopped pushing. "Thomas? Now that'll be a sight worth seeing." The two men settled at a table. "I'm glad I came," said James. "This Australia is quite beautiful. I envisioned it desert-like…barren, but it's so green.

"Desert's the other side," said John.

"So…you and Louise, eh? What are the odds of that?" Sadie came and sat down at the table. "Introduce me, John, "she said.

"James this is Sadie Blackburn…Sadie, meet James Mannington."

"You look just like my first husband, Mr. Mannington. I could listen to you talk all day, love the accent," she said. The two shook hands across the table.

"So, how many times have you been married?" James asked.

"Never," Sadie replied and gave him the full effect of her smile. "Sadie owns this hotel and runs a few sheep…keeps her out of trouble," said John

"Why are you in the wheel-chair?" said Sadie. She was so direct it caught James off guard. Everyone had always avoided mentioning the wheelchair or his affliction and here was this woman asking him out right. He liked that. "I was shot during the war."

"So, after the war, what did you do?" James looked a little guilty. "Nothing," he said. He saw Sadie's eyes widen in disbelief. She laughed, "What do you mean nothing? It's only your legs that don't work. An educated man like you could do so many things. We need schoolteachers, accountants, a new editor for the newspaper."

"Sadie, James is a…"

"No, it's all right John, I can take it from here," said James. James was fascinated with this woman. She didn't pity him as did so many others.

"I have to get back to the barbershop," said John, "so you'll excuse me if I dash off? I'll talk to you later, James," John was totally ignored. James and Sadie had forgotten he was there. "Right, I'll go then," said John and picked up his hat and headed for the door. James leaned towards Sadie. "What about dinner," he said.

"We serve dinner at 8.p.m. sharp."

"No, I mean, what about you having dinner with me…just us. I'd like to get to know you better, Sadie Blackburn. You're an extraordinary woman. Not like anyone I've ever met before."

Sadie put her hand to her throat. "I don't think it would look right to be having dinner with the guests and in front of the staff."

"Oh, I see," said James and nodded his understanding.

"But," said Sadie, "I have my own quarters with a dining room. We could have dinner there."

"Louise, what shall I wear? I haven't had dinner alone with a man since…and what about my hair, look at it! I look like a scarecrow."

Louise was rummaging through Sadie's wardrobe. "This will be perfect for you, try it on." She handed Sadie a plain black dress with a sweetheart neckline.

"He'll ask me who died if I show up in that thing!"

"You've got that beautiful star shaped brooch your father gave you… the diamond one. Simple but elegant."

"They're not real diamonds," said Sadie. "He's so handsome, Louise, and I'm so plain. He's educated and all I know is the hotel and sheep. We're so different. Look at my hair, Louise, it's all over the place…my hands are shaking. I feel like a bloody sixteen year old."

Louise laughed. "You'll be fine and you're not plain, Sadie. You can nip down to the hairdresser and get your hair done, there's plenty of time."

"What will I say to him? How should I act? I've forgotten how to do this, Louise."

"Calm down. You just have to be yourself. You seem to have impressed him this morning."

"I was nervous. You know how I am when I get nervous…I blurt things out, I make jokes." Sadie put on the dress and looked at herself in the mirror. "Mutton dressed like lamb…that's what I feel like! The dress doesn't look bad on me, though." Sadie opened a drawer and took out the brooch and held it above her left breast.

"Wear it on the left side… at the waist," said Louise. "You don't want to draw attention away from the neckline." Sadie repositioned the brooch. "Not bad. In fact I have some earrings that go with the brooch. Pair of black shoes and I'm all set. Thank you, Louise."

"If you're nervous about conversation ask him questions about himself."

"Yes, that's a good idea, I can do that. I don't know why I'm getting into such a tizz woz…it's only dinner, isn't it?"

At eight o'clock Sadie opened the door to James. She put one foot in front of the other and posed at the door. Her hair was freshly washed and coiffed, the black dress fitted her figure well and the brooch and earrings glittered.

"You look beautiful," said James.

Sadie lowered her eyes. "I've never been beautiful even on my best day, Mr. Mannington."

James reached for her hand and kissed it. "Call me James. Believe me, Sadie, you look stunning." Not used to receiving compliments Sadie said nothing in reply. She led James to the table with its fresh flowers, white tablecloth and wine glasses.

"Some Australian wine," she said. "Bet you've never tried our wine. Red, we're having beef."

James never took his eyes off Sadie as she poured the wine then sat down opposite him. There was no conversation. Sadie recalled Louise's advice.

"James, tell me three things you'd like me to know about you?" Sadie said and cocked her head to one side. James looked thoughtful for a moment then with a slight smile said, "I'd like you to know I believe in love at first sight, that my intentions are honorable and…that I'm not impotent, despite the legs." Sadie was stunned for a moment but then burst out laughing.

"You *know* it crossed your mind," said James.

"Yes it did," said Sadie but she was glowing at the thought of his first two answers.

"I've wasted my life," said James, his expression serious, "feeling sorry for myself. I'm not about to let another opportunity slip by. I'm more aware and appreciative of everything since I let go of the bitterness. It's the first time I've admitted that. Tell me, Sadie, what are the three things you'd like me to know about you?"

"Oh, no, no, no…I ask the questions?"

"Come on, tell me."

"Well, if you must know, I'm stubborn, have a bit of a temper now and then and…" she put her elbow on the table, her chin in her hand, "I think you're the handsomest and most charming man I've ever known this side of heaven."

"You only answered two of the questions. What's the third thing you'd like me to know about you?"

"That I, too, believe in love at first sight."

CHAPTER FOURTEEN
Kitchen Confrontations

John leaned against the sink and watched Louise. The kitchen was a beehive of activity as she rushed from one task to the next.

"May I ask why you wear the apron on your behind and not in front? Looks a bit odd," said John.

"Isn't it obvious? I wipe my hands on my behind!" Louise demonstrated. She was agitated.

"Damn! It always lumps and sticks to the bottom," she complained and thrashed a wooden spoon inside a saucepan.

"Custard," she said, anticipating John's next question and slid the pan off the burner to cool. Louise turned and poked two fingers into bread dough that had been left to rise in a yellow-ware bowl. She opened the door of the oven and pulled out a golden crusted loaf, she'd made earlier, then banged the door shut with her shoe. Louise tapped the loaf, listening to the hollow sound it made. She seemed satisfied with its doneness and turned it out of the tin and onto the table. The aroma of the fresh baked bread filled the kitchen. Judging by the flour in her hair and on the floor, and several cupboard doors that had been left open as Louise searched for ingredients, John suspected the bread had put up quite a battle.

"Don't you have somewhere to be?" Louise asked her voice full of impatience.

"Not going anywhere until I get a piece of that bread," said John.
Louise looked at him. He was wearing a dark navy shirt with sleeves rolled up to the elbows and light khaki trousers. His thumbs were looped behind brown leather braces and he wore a wide- brimmed hat.

"Can't you see the mess I'm in?" Louise waved her arms to indicate the kitchen.

"Sadie will be here any minute," she continued, "I don't have time to…"

John removed his hat and glared at her in mock determination. He hooked his foot around the leg of a chair and slid it forward.

"Oh, sit down then!" Louise opened a concealed drawer in the table. She withdrew a serrated- edged knife then cut through the hot bread and handed a generous slice to John. His mouth full he nodded his approval.

"I'm just nervous about the wedding, I suppose. I didn't mean to take it out on you. What was the outcome of your conversation with James Mannington?"

"He wants Declan to be schooled in England but I told him it's too soon."

"I meant did you and James resolve your differences?"

"We got along fine. Did you know he was the one who had the telegram sent telling us where Declan was?"

"No. I thought it just came through the office."

"You'll be interested to learn that James has decided to work for The Agency. He wants to make improvements to the system. That's the penance he's assigned to himself. He asked for another chance. Not easy for one man to apologize to another you know? You'll see him tomorrow, I've invited him here. Thought it might be a good place for him to get to know Declan. He's anxious to pick your brain about what can be changed at The Agency."

"I'm glad the two of you have sorted it out. Have you thought about asking him to be your best man? You still don't have one. I think it would be nice to make this a family affair."

"Louise, Phoebe will be coming here after the wedding. How will you feel about that? Knowing I…"

Louise rubbed the back of John's hand and smiled at him. "She's Declan's mother. She has a right to see her son. We *have* to make this work, John, there are three children counting on us. What were you thinking…I'd be jealous?" Her laughter sounded false to her.

"I thought perhaps you'd feel… uncomfortable." Louise scoffed at the suggestion. Although she had never seen Phoebe Mannington she imagined her to be elegant, poised and beautiful. Louise suddenly felt self-conscious. She fussed with her hair and plucked at the ties of her apron to remove it. In her present appearance she wondered if John was making comparisons between the two.

"Well, I need to get back to my baking and I'm sure you have a dozen things you need to do." John sensed a tension in her voice and stood up. He was just putting on his hat when Sadie thrust her head inside the door.

"Hello. I did knock but you must not have heard me. Am I interrupting something?" Sadie asked, looking from one to the other.

"Course not. I was just leaving," said John and did just that.

"Come on in Sadie, we were just discussing… the wedding," Louise lied.

Sadie put a dish on the table. "Bread pudding," she said. "Mum's got a packet of Bird's custard powder, in the cupboard somewhere, to go with it. I'll make it if you like."

Louise was ashamed at the state the kitchen was in and sounded short and formal. "Do sit down, Sadie. Mum already had me make the custard. It's done. I'll put the kettle on." The two women sat down at the table. Tea was poured into bone china cups.

"What is it, Louise? You and John getting wedding jitters?"

"I don't know what's the matter with me, I'm just a bit edgy that's all. How am I going to make all this work, Sadie. I've never raised children before. I look a mess and I'm so… tired. Maybe I'm not cut out for this."

"Don't be silly. You're still adjusting to the climate. The heat takes it out of you and getting married…well it's bound to get your nerves on edge a bit isn't it?" Louise gave a deep sigh and looked out the window.

"Come on, Louise, what's all this really about?" said Sadie.

"Phoebe Mannington will be coming here, after the wedding, and look at me. How do I compete with someone like her?"

"Compete? Whatever gave you the idea that you're competing with Phoebe Mannington?"

"Because not once has John ever told me he loves me," she whispered. Louise looked at Sadie with tear-filled eyes. Sadie was silent for a moment. "That doesn't mean anything…he asked you to marry him didn't he?"

"Perhaps he still has feelings for Phoebe but because she's married…"

"Don't be daft woman. You're being irrational. It's just the pre-wedding nerves that's all."

"I suppose you're right. I don't know what's wrong with me today."

"*I've* got something that'll cheer you up?" said Sadie.

"What is it?" Louise returned the kettle to the hob.

"A letter for you…from England." Sadie removed it from her pocket and waved it in the air. Louise grabbed it. "It's from Elizabeth," she said and tore it open.

"She got married! Finally said yes to Archie. They got married a month ago and she says she'll be here for the wedding. Oh, my God, I've got loads to do Sadie…*Elizabeth's coming*…I can't believe it. Isn't it wonderful?"

"Wish I'd have given you the letter yesterday!" said Sadie. "I suppose I'd better give you a hand to get finished up here or we'll never get that last fitting done on the dress."

John stood on the front porch and smoked a cigarette and wondered what he'd said to cause the undercurrent of tenseness in Louise.

It was a warm day with a light breeze. Mum was sitting in one of the old rockers, the soft rhythmic clicking of her knitting needles the only sound. Alice was napping on a patch of grass in the front yard. The child lay half on the blanket, her behind in the air and knees drawn up under her. Her bottle lay under her hand. Milk dripped from the teat and onto the grass. She stirred, stretched out her fingers and, once reassured the bottle was still there, fell back asleep. Kate sat on the steps of the porch reading a book of Little Women that Mum had given her. Declan sat on the rail of the porch, his knees up and his head back against a wooden support post. He leaned his head forward slightly and watched a bird as it circled above. He shaded his eyes with both hands to get a better look at it. Declan watched the bird circling. It must have spotted a rodent or a lizard, he thought. He looked down to see what had caught its attention and saw something that froze his blood.

There wasn't time…there wasn't going to be time, he thought. Declan stiffened his body and snapped his fingers to get John's attention, yet never took his eyes from Alice.

"What is it?" said John, his voice low as he sensed something was wrong. Declan put his finger to his lips and whispered, "Snake, next to Alice." The shock of hearing Declan speak was equal only to the words '*snake*' and '*Alice*' in the same sentence.

John's mother didn't move. Her first instinct was to cry out and rush to the child and gather her up but she knew she mustn't. The snake was too close. If Alice woke up and moved…the Tiger snake was highly venomous.

Kate looked up from her book and sucked in her breath. She gripped the edges of the book when she saw the snake.

"Don't any of you move," John whispered and turned on his heel back into the house. "What is it?" said Louise seeing the purposeful look on his face.

"Stay put and keep quiet," John said to both women. He went straight to the revolver that was kept in the upper kitchen cupboard, behind a small black cashbox. He moved fast to retrieve it. He checked the chambers and removed the safety while he walked.

"Oh my God what is it? The children are out there," whispered Louise. John ignored her. The last time the gun had been out of the cupboard was to shoot a trio of marauding Dingoes that came during lambing season.

The Tiger snake had come out of the shade under the porch. Its forked tongue flicked in and out to taste odors in the air. It side- winded its way across the cool grass towards the spilled milk, its striped body reticulating towards the sleeping child. Alice's pudgy hand was inches away, well within striking distance. She opened her eyes. If she grasped the bottle…

"*Jesus!*" whispered John under his breath. He had fired many a shot with a steady hand during the war but now found his hand shook. He stood at the edge of the porch and aimed, sucked in a breath and held it…then squeezed the trigger and fired.

The snake, wounded, writhed, twisted and coiled back on itself. Declan saw the opportunity and dropped from the porch rail. He grabbed the screaming Alice and yanked her by her wrist away from the snake.
Louise and Sadie came running outside.

"Declan, get her clear!" shouted John. "It's not dead!" John's second shot took the snake's head off.

Alice had screamed at the first shot and clung to Declan. The second shot she screamed louder and wrapped her dimpled arms around Declan's neck. She held on tight and refused to let go even when Louise and Sadie tried to take the child from him. Mum checked Alice's hands and arms to make sure the snake hadn't struck.

"I don't see anything," she said over her shoulder and managed to take Alice from Declan. Alice hung on to her grandmother like a limpet.

"Are you alright?" asked John, directing his question at the boy.
Declan nodded.

"Better get some of the men back here. If there was one there'll be more. We'll need to check it out." Declan started to run.

"*Declan!*" shouted John, his voice as abrupt as the shots he'd just fired. "You spoke...you bloody well spoke!" Declan stopped for a moment, looked back and grinned. "I know. I'll be right back."

CHAPTER FIFTEEN
The Wedding

On the day of the wedding, in a room at the Blackburn Hotel, Louise looked at her reflection in the mirror. The dress was a beautiful white satin with short flared sleeves. It had a three-quarter length fish-tail hem with a square necked bodice. The white summer hat was wide-brimmed with the front turned up and the back down, the fabric delicate. The white gave a contrasting background to the dark curls that framed Louise's face. The back of her hair had been pinned at the nape of her neck. White stockings and matching, low-heeled 'Mary Jane' shoes completed the picture. Louise was just putting on the pearl earrings Mum had given her as a wedding present, when Sadie walked into the room. She gasped and put her fingers to her lips. What she wouldn't have given, Sadie thought, to have had her fiancé see *her* in that dress. Her eyes brimmed with tears.

Louise read her thoughts and crossed the room to put her arms around her.

"I know…I know," Louise said, immediately understanding the woman's sadness.

Sadie turned around, blew her nose into an embroidered handkerchief and waved her hand to indicate she was to be ignored.

She stuck the handkerchief up her sleeve and in a rush of words turned back to Louise and said, "Anyway, I assume you've got something old, something new or blue or something? How does that saying go?"

Louise realizing that Sadie wanted to get past the moment, contributed with, "Yes! Earrings, the dress, old horseshoe for luck and a blue hanky." She pointed to each item. The horseshoe had been painted white and hung from a ribbon.

"Have you got something new?" Sadie asked.

"Yes, I have…*you*!" said Louise. "My new best friend."

"Now don't get me crying all over again. Have you got sixpence in your shoe for good luck?"

"Two," said Louise. "One in each shoe." Both women laughed.

Sadie became quiet and in a serious tone said," Better let me take that. I'll give it back to you later." Louise followed Sadie's gaze and looked down at her left hand. David's ring. She'd worn it for so long it had become part of her. She slipped it off and gave it to Sadie. Sadie and Louise stood in silence for a moment looking at each other.

"It's *time*," said Sadie, her words emphasizing the double meaning to Louise. "Time to put David behind you, now, and time to get to the church. You look so beautiful Louise. Oh 'S truth!" A look of horror crossed Sadie's face. "I can't believe it. I forgot to bring the flowers. We'll grab them on the way to the church. Wait 'til you see them, Louise, white roses with bits of green fern."

"How did you get roses way out here?"

"They do well out here, I'll have you know."

"If anyone had told me I'd be living in Australia, married and with three children, all in the space of months, I'd have called them mad," said Louise. Sadie smiled. "Not many get a second chance at happiness. Now then, let's get a move on. There won't be a dry eye in the house after everyone gets a look at you in that dress. I like that James Mannington, by the way. Nice bloke. Good looking too."

John pushed James up the wooden ramp and into the church.

"It was kind of you to provide such an easy access for me John."

"Don't get too fond of it we have to have the ramp back for the sheep dip enclosure." James grabbed John's sleeve and stopped him inside the church. "All joking aside, John. Thank you for everything. It's *all* going to work out you know. Phoebe's made some drastic changes. She's happy. George will be good to the boy…he's that kind of man. I promise you, Declan will get the best education and I'll bring him back every summer. He'll get the best of both our worlds, John."

"I know he will," John said.

"John?"

"What?"

"That Sadie Blackburn," said James.

"What about her?" John replied.

"Wouldn't *she* be a breath of fresh air at Baden Hall?"

"You can't be serious?" said John.

98

"I *might* be. I like the way she talks to me…cheeky…direct. She doesn't pity me. She's a handsome woman and I think she likes me."

"But you've only known her a few days," said John, "and what about your family titles?"

"I've changed. I know what's *really* important now."

"Huh! You and Sadie are as different as chalk and cheese," said John.

"I'll be back and forth with Declan," said James. "We'll just have to see what comes of it, won't we."

The church was a fairly small building with white clapboard siding. The English ancestors of the community had built it in a style they'd remembered from back home as they tried to recreate the old country in the new. The steeple housed a hand-forged bell. Steps led to simply carved double doors that graced the front of the church. It was cool inside. There was a buzz of conversation as the people visited. Declan, Kate and Alice entered the church just before the bride. As Louise came into the vestry Declan said, "You look *very* pretty."

"You look *beautiful,* Louise," said Kate. Alice held her arms out thinking Louise was going to pick her up but Kate took her hand. Louise bent down and kissed each one of the children on the cheek.

"I love you all and I promise we're going to be *very* happy," she said and meant it.

Mrs. Pierce, the organist, spotted the bride on the arm of Dr. Phillips at the back of the church. This was her cue. In her haste she hit a note off key, looked apologetic and then began again. Mrs. Pierce was a very short heavy-set woman who could barely reach the pedals. Nothing could be seen of her but elbows, back and feet as she furiously worked the keys, pedals and stops of the organ. Her appearance was that of someone frantically trying to save herself from drowning.

On the second chorus Mrs. Pierce's shrill voice, much to the surprise of out of towners, belted out the words to '*Here comes the Bride.*" The locals, not the least bit surprised joined in and sang, in solemn voices, as though singing a hymn.

"She used to play in a pub of an evening, back in England." Doctor Phillips whispered to Louise from the corner of his mouth. That would explain how Mrs. Pierce managed to make it a sing-a-long, thought Louise and tried hard not to smile. Everyone stood and turned as the bride came down the aisle. The sight of her took John Reynolds breath away. The church was crowded, some even stood. The side aisles and back of the church were packed. Louise stood beside John in front of the Vicar. The Vicar chatted for a second or two while the congregation got settled. "Any questions?" he whispered.

"Yes, just one," said Louise. John and the Vicar looked at Louise intently.

"Do you love me?" Louise said to John.

"What are you talking about woman? I asked you to marry me didn't I? I thought it was understood."

"But you've never once *said* you loved me."

"I must have!" said John.

Louise was insistent. "Not once," she said. The congregation was silent, straining to hear what was being said.

"Bit late to bring this up now isn't it?" said the Vicar. John looked thoughtful for a moment then turned to face the congregation. He spread his arms wide. "I *love* this woman," he shouted. He turned to Louise.

"I love you...satisfied?" John kissed her. "I love you," he repeated.

Everyone stood up and applauded. A sea of handkerchiefs emerged and dabbed at the eyes of most of the women.

"Are you ready *now*," said the Vicar and glared at Louise, daring her to say no. Louise nodded her head. Her eyes were bright and she looked at John with all the love in her heart.

"I'm ready," she said.

"Good!" said the Vicar. "Then let's get on with it."

"Dearly beloved, we are gathered here today..." The ceremony continued.

"Do you, John Alphonse Reynolds..." Louise turned to John who deliberately looked straight ahead.

"*Alphonse?*" she whispered.

"It was my uncles name. The one who left me the station," he said without moving his lips. Louise lowered her head so that her hat might hide her smile.

"*Now what?*" said the Vicar looking slightly annoyed.

"Nothing," said John. "Carry on."

The new Mr. and Mrs. Reynolds came out of the church and into the bright sunshine. Everyone cheered and patted John on the back. The women clustered about the bride and hugged her.

"Toss the bouquet!" they shouted.

Louise pulled out a single rose to keep then tossed the bouquet right into the hands of Sadie Blackburn.

Sadie glanced down at James who sat in his chair beside her. "Better watch yourself," she said and winked at James.

"Fancy yourself as the next Lady Mannington do you?"

"Titles don't mean much here, in this country, but a good looking man... now *that's* something altogether different." James laughed. "I *like* you Sadie Blackburn," he said.

In the evening light a long shadow fell across Maggie's grave. Louise placed the rose she'd saved from her bouquet, that day, in front of the headstone.

"I know that he'll *always* love *you*," she said "but he's managed to make room in his heart for me too, Maggie. I'll be a good wife to him and I love the children as though they were my own. I just wanted you to know that." Louise folded her arms and began to walk back towards the house then stopped... "I'm going to have a baby of my own, Maggie. I think Mum suspects but I've not told John yet."

The budgerigars, disturbed by Maggie's presence, twittered in the trees and from nowhere a warm breeze came up and caressed Louise's cheek, then was gone as quickly as it came. Louise stepped back, folded her arms and walked slowly down the hill towards home.

CHAPTER SIXTEEN
Decisions

The hotel restaurant was almost empty. The square tables were covered with crisp white tablecloths and Mary moved from one to the next filling the silver-plated salt-cellars. It was mid- afternoon and too early for the dinner crowd.

Louise added milk and sugar to the steaming black tea that she poured into a white china cup. She stirred it then took a sip and closed her eyes. She'd volunteered to help out at the surgery while Doctor Phillips was out of town. It had been a long day. Sadie's offer of tea was a welcome break. She wasn't going to rush it for anything.

"Well, what do you think?" said Sadie and glanced around the room to make sure she hadn't been overheard.

Louise studied her friend for a moment. "Depends…do you love him?"

"I do but we're so…different. I never expected him to ask me to come to England and marry him, did I?"

Louise sighed. "You're the first person he wants to see when he comes to get Declan. Lord knows, you could wallpaper this whole place with the letters James sends you."

"And that's another thing…what am I supposed to do with the hotel?"

"Come on, Sadie, Mary practically runs this place. You taught her yourself. She can manage it for you. You wouldn't have to sell it."

"But there's that big house of his, however would I manage?"

"Running Baden Hall isn't such a far stretch from running the hotel…except you'd be mistress of the house."

"*Mistress of the house*." Sadie rolled the words out slowly. "Lady Mannington. Can you imagine it…me, plain old Sadie Blackburn… spinster, a titled lady." She laughed nervously.

"What will his friends think of me? I won't fit in, Louise." Sadie looked overwhelmed by the thought of it all.

"That's not it, is it Sadie? You've never worried about what people thought of you before."

"I'm out of his class…a peasant compared to what he's used to." Louise laughed. "If James had wanted someone stuffy and proper he'd have found her in England. He liked you, from the start, because you didn't pity him. You're outspoken and you bring out the best in him. He loves you."

"Well, I do think about him all the time," said Sadie.

"Then what's to consider?" Sadie looked off into the distance for a moment.

"You're right, there is nothing to consider, is there?" Her eyes blazed and her chin came up. "Do you think I'm too old to wear that wedding dress; it's been stored in mothballs for ages?"

"The truth?" said Louise. "Yes."

"I was afraid you'd say that. Then, what do you say we take a trip to Melbourne, next week? You can help me look for a nice frock or a decent suit."

"So, this means you're going to tell him yes?"

Without hesitation Sadie said, "I am."

Louise spilled her tea as she clattered the cup back on the saucer and squealed with delight. She grabbed Sadie's hand and squeezed it across the table.

"It's an awful long way to England," said Sadie.

"Declan and Kate are going anyway. You can travel with them."

"That's true," said Sadie. "I can't believe how grown up those two are. I wish Kate wasn't leaving. Willoughby won't be the same without her."

"I know, but she's finished her training in Sydney. She's had it in her head to go back to England and reclaim her parents' home since I met her. There's nothing I can say to stop her, I've tried. She's convinced her brother, Harry, will find his way back there at some point. I did try to help her find him but, when he was adopted, the records were sealed."

"I think Kate's going to make a wonderful nurse," said Sadie.

"She will. I was glad I could pull a few strings for her in England. I shall miss her."

"Well it's not like she'll be gone for good and I'll be over there to keep an eye on her, won't I?"

"They're both leaving me at once," said Louise. She looked wistful for a moment. "Seems like only yesterday that Declan was a hollow-eyed, undernourished little scruff of a boy."

"But that was a long time ago, Louise. He works hard as any man and look at him, all filled out and such a handsome boy." Louise thought about Declan. He was tall like his father and had the same good looks. He was serious and articulate and had acquired a formal English accent. Declan had excelled at the school in England. The once reclusive child had grown into a confident young man. No longer was he the small boy who stiffened his whole body each time Louise tried to hug him. With Mum, whom he called Gran, he had an easy way about him and a sense of humour. Though he'd grown quiet around Kate, lately, he was generous with his affection towards his sisters Alice and Margaret. Louise insisted her daughter be named after Maggie. Sadie was right about Declan. He looked so much older than his years and didn't seem to need anything or anyone.

Sadie patted Louise's hand. "You've been a good mother to those children. You've done right by them. They can easily function in this world without you if they had to. You'll still have Alice and Margaret at home. Those God-daughters of mine are going to be quite a handful when they get a bit older."

Louise expelled a deep sigh.

"Come on, Louise, this is supposed to be a happy time. I'm getting married, for goodness sakes! *Mary*, bring us another pot of tea, will you love, and a couple of wedges of that Victoria Sandwich cake."

Louise smiled and visibly relaxed.

"Declan's got a crush on Kate, you know," said Sadie. Louise raised an eyebrow.

"You mark my words, he's got a thing for Kate."

"That's ridiculous! He always seems irritated with her. Besides she's older than him." Sadie cocked her head to one side, widened her eyes, and gave an all knowing look.

Mary came to the table with a fresh pot of tea. Louise smiled at her.

When she left Sadie said, "That girl...I'm glad you brought her to Willoughby. She's like my own family."

"Still can't get over the change in her. If you'd seen her when I first did…"

"She has a young man now…Daniel. He's solid, hard worker and quite the gentleman. They'll do well together. Everyone's growing up, Louise. Time doesn't stand still for anyone."

"No, it doesn't," said Louise with a sigh as she thought about Declan and Kate.

CHAPTER SEVENTEEN
Second Thoughts

Kate and Sadie shared a cabin on the trip over to England. The closer the ship got to Southampton the more nervous Sadie became. As she and Kate lounged in canvas deck chairs they watched the seagulls as they soared and dipped on the winds as they followed the ship.

Sadie said, "I'm a nervous wreck about all this. I've never been out of Australia and I don't know a soul in England. I'm already homesick and I'm not even there yet."

Kate snapped her book shut, unable to concentrate with Sadie rattling on. "Once you see James you'll be fine," said Kate. "It's been years since I've been to England so it'll be an adjustment for me too." She leaned over and squeezed Sadie's hand. "I'll come up and see you…and Declan will be there." Declan appeared in front of the two women. Kate shaded her eyes to look up at him.

"Want to walk with me around the deck? You can just see land," he said.

"You two go ahead," said Sadie. "Think I'll just stay here and vegetate a bit." She leaned her head back and closed her eyes. Kate swung her legs round and got up. She fell into step beside Declan. "She's having second thoughts," said Kate.

"I wish you were," said Declan. Kate stopped and turned towards him. A gust of wind almost lifted her hat off. She placed her hand on top of it to hold it on.

"I mean it Kate," said Declan. "You're making a big mistake going back to England and for what? Harry may not even be alive and there's a good chance he may never return to that house, let alone remember who *you* are." Declan stood a head taller than Kate. She poked him in the chest with her finger.

"Who are *you* to tell me what I should and shouldn't do? You're just a boy. You have no concept of how much it matters to me that I find Harry. I know he'll come back to that house."

"What are you going to do if he doesn't, waste your life and wait forever? Seems pretty stupid to me. You belong back in Willoughby not gallivanting halfway across the world on a 'what if'."

"Stupid is it? Let me tell you, Declan Reynolds, you've been a thorn in my side for the last two years. You've never approved of *anything* I've done. Going to Sydney was a mistake, in your eyes. Going back to England, living by myself…you've turned into such a brat. Probably all the airs and graces you've acquired living with your Uncle James and going to that posh school. I think someone needs to take you down a peg or two!" Kate walked off in search of Sadie, her face hot with anger.

"Oh this old thing, you're joking," said Sadie in answer to James's compliment on the blue floral dress she was wearing. "I've had it for *years*." Kate rolled her eyes upward. They'd shopped for days just to find the perfect dress, in Melbourne, for her meeting with James.

"Come in…all of you," said James. "Glad to have you back Declan and look at *you* Kate," he marveled. "What a stunning looking woman you turned out to be. We'll have a hard time keeping all the young men away, I can tell you." Declan muttered something under his breath. James reached for Sadie's hand to kiss. She tried to pull it back but he wouldn't let go. Her un-manicured hands were rough from years of hard work. There were dark sun spots on the back, the skin deeply tanned. James kissed the back of her hand and then her palm. No-one had ever kissed her hand before. It embarrassed and delighted Sadie.

As they entered the hallway Sadie looked around in awe. Instead of admiring the elegance and grandeur, she marveled at how such high windows stayed so spotlessly clean.

"Nothing to concern yourself about, all that's taken care of," said James. Sadie drifted into the dining room. The table was set for dinner with crystal glasses for water and wine. She noted the multiple sets of utensils, chargers under the plates, and gravy boats. "I only cook plain food, you know. Can't imagine cod and chips with mushy peas on these plates."

"Cook does all that…and we have servants."

Sadie was impressed. "So, what is it, exactly, that *I* do?"

"Oh, I'm sure we'll find *something* for you to do," said James and laughed.

Sadie and James decided to get married at the registry office, in London, with only Kate and Declan in attendance.

"You don't know what you're letting yourself in for," said Sadie.

"Neither do you, "said James.

Declan returned to school. Kate re-opened the empty house on Broad Street and presented herself to the hospital for duty. Sadie, afraid of how James's friends would receive her found, to her relief, that they were fascinated with her life in Australia. She became involved in local projects. Not the outsider she thought she'd be, Sadie was welcomed and embraced into the community. She helped prepare meals with cook and would often be caught down on her hands and knees polishing the daylights out of the front hallway floor.

"*Lady Mannington*, what *are* you doing?" James would tease when he saw her down on all fours with her behind in the air, polishing the oak floors. "I love this place, James, I appreciate old things. They need to be taken care of. Imagine all the work that went into this place all those years ago. You don't find quality like this anymore."

"The only old thing you need to appreciate and take care of…is me," said James and laughed.

CHAPTER EIGHTEEN
A Coming of Age

Declan felt refined and sophisticated in the new black tuxedo his Uncle James had bought him for the dinner to be held in honour of his twenty-first birthday. He stood in the hallway, at the foot of the stairs, and fiddled with the white bow-tie. He loved spending time at Baden Hall but didn't think of it as home. He was homesick for Willoughby. There'd be a few guests tonight but the only one he cared about seeing was Kate. She'd be a little late as she'd pulled a double shift at the hospital. She told Sadie she could stay for the whole weekend, though. Kate had turned into a beautiful woman. Her long hair, braided and wrapped around her head when she was on duty, was worn loose or hung in one plait down the centre of her back when she wasn't working. Declan never tired of looking at her.

"You look quite the man about town," said Sadie, interrupting his thoughts as she walked in a circle around Declan. "Very nice indeed."

"You're going to give the boy a big head if you keep complimenting him," said James, in amusement, wheeling himself into the hall.

"He has your good looks, James," said Sadie winking at Declan.

"Oh, I don't know about that," said James, obviously pleased at the compliment.

Sadie kissed Declan's cheek. "Happy birthday, love. Got a few things to do before your guests arrive. See you later."

When they were left alone James said, sheepishly, "She knows how to manipulate me, that woman."

"You'd be lost without her, Uncle James, and you know it." James waved his hand, dismissing the remark. "Come to the study with me. We'll have a drink together, just the two of us. I want to talk to you about something." After Declan poured two whiskeys and handed one to his uncle, James wasted no time.

"I think this is going to be a long, dragged out war, Declan. I know you've a mind to go and believe me that's commendable but..." Declan sat down then leaned forward to rest his forearms on his knees. He held the glass in both hands and studied the golden liquid inside. He and his uncle had had this conversation before.

"You and my father didn't hesitate when the call came." Declan stood up and walked to the window with glass in hand.

"Just hear me out," said James. "I've got contacts. I can keep you out of harm's way. You'll get a commission...war offices with Winston Churchill no less."

"I've made up my mind, Uncle James. I don't want to sit the war out behind a desk."

"But you're the last of two family lines; this estate...Willoughby. If something happens to you it will all be lost... generations of work and tradition for nothing."

"I've already made a commitment. I was going to tell you after dinner tonight." said Declan.

"What are you talking about?" James looked intently at his nephew and leaned forward in his wheelchair. "What have you done?"

Declan turned from the window and faced James. "I start pilot training next week. I joined the R.A.F."

"You've *what*? Do you know what your chance of survival will be? You can't..."

"I've made up my mind, Uncle James. You won't talk me out of it."

James seemed visibly deflated. He slumped in his chair and took a sip of the whiskey. After a moment of silence he said, "I remember standing in that exact spot making the same argument to *my* father. For the first time I understand how *he* felt when he asked me not to go. Have you told your Dad?"

"No. I'll telephone him tomorrow."

"No need," said James, his voice subdued, "he's here."

"Dad's *here*?"

"Whole family, your Gran too. Part of your birthday present...their idea."

"Where are they?"

"Waiting to surprise you at dinner…sounds as though you're the one with the surprise, though. They're not going to be happy about this."

"But you'll be there to back me up," said Declan, confidence in his voice. A gong sounded. "Dinner," said James. "I was supposed to keep you busy in here while your guests were seated. Act surprised when you see the family."

"I won't be acting," said Declan. When James and Declan entered the dining hall everyone yelled *"Surprise!"* Around the long table stood John, Louise, Margaret and Alice, Gran, Phoebe and George and three of Declan's college friends Alec, Michael, Colin…and Kate.

Declan's face registered what looked like surprise but was, in fact, sheer joy at seeing all his favourite people in one place. He stepped forward and lifted his grandmother off the ground, rusching her skirt up at the back. "Put me down you silly lad, you'll do yerself a mischief!" she said, but kissed his cheek and struggled to pull her skirt down in the back lest her bloomers showed. Declan shook George's hand and kissed his mother and Louise on the cheek. Kate offered her cheek to Declan. He kissed it.

"Happy Birthday," she said.

"Thank you," he replied. Gran didn't miss the slight heightened colour in Kate's face. After a dinner of roast mutton with Major Grey's chutney, roast potatoes and brussel sprouts there was a birthday cake with twenty-one candles on top. Champagne was brought out in fluted glasses. Presents were opened; a scarf, gloves and a leather coin holder from Declan's college friends, a book from Alice, handkerchief, with his initials embroidered on, from Margaret and a silver St. Christopher on a chain from Kate.

"To keep you safe wherever you are," Kate said.

Gran gave him a ring in a small black velvet box. It was a single diamond surrounded by tiny pearls and rubies. "Your grandfather gave it to me when he asked me to marry him. It was his mother's. Find someone special to give it to."

Their eyes locked for a moment. "Oh, Gran," Declan said and hugged the old woman.

"There is one last gift," James announced and handed Declan a small box. "It's from your father and Louise, George and your mother and from Sadie and me."

It was no bigger than a matchbox. '*Declan Mannington Reynolds*' was printed on a gold edged label that hung from the box. Declan had no clue what it could be and when he opened it his jaw dropped. "Is this what I think it is?" he asked and held up a silver key.

"It's out in the drive-way," said James. Declan, Kate, his sisters and friends ran to the front door. There, parked at an angle, stood a two-seater cream coloured MG. The reflection of the house lights, on the body and chrome, made it a centerpiece in the driveway.

Declan gasped, strode back into the house and said. "It's really *mine*? I can't believe it. Thank you...all."

He didn't wait for a response but dashed back out to the front steps. Everyone, except Kate, had the door and boot open as they investigated the whole car. Declan stood next to Kate and was about to say something to her when Thomas came outside. He was slow and his spine a little crooked but he still continued to officiate as butler and valet.

"Your presence is requested, back in the dining room, in fifteen minutes. Yours too Miss Kate. I'll get the others."

"Wonder what that's all about?" said Kate. Declan didn't reply.

After everyone was seated, Declan stood up and walked to the head of the table. He looked at the expectant faces and cleared his throat. "I've joined the RAF, I start pilot training next week." There was utter silence in the room.

"We all joined up together," said Colin, indicating Alec and Michael. "Same squadron." John lowered his head.

"He only just sprang this on me before dinner, John. I had no idea," said James.

Kate felt as though the bottom had fallen out of her heart.

"James, you said you'd find him a desk job...something safe until the war is over," said Phoebe. "You promised."

"He wouldn't listen to me," said James.

"I'll be above it all, in the air. Nothing's going to happen to me," said Declan.

"You've no idea what you've done," said John and rose to his feet. His voice began to rise in anger. "You think it's some sort of lark. That because you're young you're invincible. That's not the way it is, Declan. In war you try to play by the civilized rules you were taught, but it's not like that out there. The enemy doesn't play by the same rules you do. It's dirty and terrifying. Ask James…ask Louise. You won't come back the same, Declan…not when you've seen what we've seen."

"You have to get him out of this, James," said Phoebe.

"No Mother, I don't want anyone to get me out of this. I won't stand by while my country is being bombed. I expect you to understand that."

There was a long silence. John moved to where Declan stood. "Look, son, I can't keep you out of this war but take advantage of what James is offering. You'll be safe."

"Nowhere in England is guaranteed safe right now. You can't expect me to sit behind a desk when my friends are out there fighting. We could lose England in this war, do you realize that? I *have* to do this, Dad. It's about duty."

John looked at his son. He wasn't a boy any longer, hadn't been for some time. He'd put up a fair argument and stood his ground. The words he'd spoken were that of a man.

"He's right," said James. "You can't argue with his principles."

"I know," said John. He looked intently at his son.

"Give me your blessing Dad and tell me you're proud of me."

Everyone's attention focused on father and son until John reached for him and held him. "I've *always* been proud of you Declan and yes, I'll give you my blessing."

"Good, that's settled then," said Gran. "Now, I think I'll have a little tipple of that Port if someone would be kind enough to pass that bottle."

Everyone laughed, the moment lightened by the old woman's remark. Her face smiled but her heart felt heavy as lead. When would the fighting ever end, Mum thought. Dad had fought in a war, then John and now her grandson. What was it with the world that there was never any peace?

Kate excused herself from the table and went outside to the driveway. Declan followed her. To Declan she looked a vision in an oyster coloured satin dress that stopped just below her knees. Her hair was loose down her back and the brown eyes glared at him.

"You're an idiot, you know? R.A.F? What were you thinking?"

"I don't want you angry at me, Kate, but it's already decided."

Kate folded her arms. "Do you know what the life expectancy of a pilot is? Would you like to visit the burn unit at the hospital and see what happens when your plane catches fire?"

"That matters to you?" His tone was sharp and his look intense. "You really care that much about me?"

Kate narrowed her eyes for a moment and looked at Declan as though for the first time. She didn't reply and pulled her arm from his grasp. As Kate went back into the house Declan called out, "I can drive you back to London tomorrow. You don't need to take the train."

"You're going too fast! *Slow down!*" said Kate as the car roared down the narrow lanes and hugged the curves in the road. Her fingers curled over the edge of her seat and her toes clenched inside her shoes. Her body was rigid against the leather.

"Stop the car! Right now! Do you hear me? I want to get out!"

Declan pulled over onto a grass verge and brought the car to a stop. Kate got out and slammed the door as hard as she could and started walking down the hedge-lined lane. She stuck her hands deep into the pockets of her coat.

"Get in the car, Kate," Declan said as he tried to catch up with her. Kate kept walking. Declan stopped her, spun her around and saw that she was crying. "Look, I'm sorry. I didn't mean to scare you. I suppose I was showing off. I've never had a car of my own before." He put his arms around her and kept repeating he was sorry.

Kate with her face against his shoulder said, "How could you be so stupid? Why did you do it?"

"I take it we're not talking about my driving?"

"You didn't have to join the R.A.F. James could have quite easily found you something safe." Declan rested his chin on the top of Kate's head. "I'm glad you worry about me, Kate."

"What if you get killed?"

He pulled away and tapped the St. Christopher that hung round his neck. "Not while I'm wearing this."

She continued to cry. "

Stop it," said Declan. "For God's sake stop crying." He kissed her hair, her face and found her lips. His mouth moved against hers. The two were unaware of anyone else in the world until a car honked as it went past them.

"Kate, nothing's going to happen to me, I promise." Declan whispered.

"You can't promise me that," she said and wiped her eyes with the heels of her hands. They walked back to the car.

Declan's leaves, from duty, were few and far between and Kate kept busy at the hospital as train-loads of incoming wounded soldiers crammed the wards. Declan and Kate met, when they could, for a weekend, a walk, conversation over a cup of tea or something stronger at the pub. One of their meetings ended in a dash for an underground train station, a designated air raid shelter. They sat across from each other in silence, listening to the explosions of bombs outside. Declan looked around at mothers clutching their children to them, old men looking towards the ceiling as though they could actually see what was happening; remembering another time and another war. Children, faces riveted in terror at the noise, had their hands clapped over their ears. A small boy played with a metal toy car. Declan reached for Kate's hand as dust particles fell and the ground shook in the subway tunnel.

"I heard tell," said one old man speaking slowly and huddled over his cane, "that undergrounds aren't very safe places to be. Don't know how true it is but the Air Warden told me one of the tunnels got a direct hit. Packed with people it was...no survivors. He said they had to fill it in with ..."

"Shut up!" said Declan. "Can't you see there are children here?"

"Now, *I* was told," said an American soldier as he offered around cigarettes," that the Germans have a sense of humour."

"How's that?" said the old man, his watery opaque eyes wide with interest.

"Seems you Limeys built a life-sized aerodrome out of wood. The planes and buildings...the whole lot a wooden decoy." The American snapped a lighter, lit cigarettes and offered gum to the children. He laughed out loud. "Jerry knew about it and dropped a non-explosive wooden bomb on it." The old man cackled with laughter that developed into a hacking cough. He spat down on the tracks. Soon the eerie wail of the siren signaled the all clear.

As Kate and Declan emerged from the tunnel and walked through the chaos of rubble, towards Kate's house, Declan put his arm around her waist and kissed the top of her head.

"I've loved you since I was about fourteen years old," he said. "Did you know that?"

"No. I thought you hated me. I never knew how I felt about you until your twenty-first birthday. That's when I saw you for the first time as a man and not just the boy I grew up with. The moment you said you'd joined up I knew I didn't ever want to be separated from you. It was as though what I felt for you had always been there, inside me, but I didn't recognize it until that day."

"Gran always knew how I felt. I tell her everything,"

Declan had been to Kate's house several times. It was a two story row house. The front door opened to reveal a long hallway with a staircase. A large living room with bay window led off to the left, a kitchen and small dining room were at the back of the house. In the small back garden an outhouse; upstairs three bedrooms and a bathroom.

"Take off your coat. All I've got is tea or cocoa, no sugar. I'll put the kettle on," said Kate. Declan walked into the front living room. It was simply furnished but clean and smelled of lavender polish. The focal point of the room was a fireplace with its typical black iron hood and surrounding blue and white Delph tiles. A brown couch faced the fireplace. The cushions had seen better days. The plainness of the room was relieved by green Jacobean patterned wallpaper. A brass fender prevented hot coals from falling towards the carpet. On one side of the fireplace sat a large chair that matched the couch. On the other side was a console wireless. Fiddling with the knobs and after much static and whining, Declan managed to find some music. Kate came in carrying a tray she put down on the sideboard in the bay window. She drew the heavy curtains.

"I'm surprised someone hasn't come along and married you before now." Declan said as he watched her. Kate was pouring milk into two tea cups. Over her shoulder she said, "There really wasn't anyone I was serious about, never had the time."

"I can't believe that," said Declan. Kate handed him tea and they both sat on the couch. Her mouth curled into a smile. "I'll admit there was Sergeant Murphy."

"Murphy?" Declan parroted the name.

"He was quite a charmer. He claimed it was love at first sight as soon as he set his eyes on me. He used the same line on all the other nurses. He was full of himself in front of his mates. What a letch he was. He *was* badly hurt, though." Kate clicked her tongue in sympathy but continued to smile.

Declan said, "Why do I have the feeling that there's more to this story?"

"There is. I ended the 'affair' by putting a steel bedpan in the ice-cold snow overnight. Slid it under him the next morning," Kate laughed out loud.

"It was all over after that. He was so embarrassed he'd cringe under the sheets when he saw me coming." Declan roared with laughter.

A soft tune came on the wireless.

"Want to dance," said Declan.

"Don't be silly, *here*?"

"Why not?" Declan took her cup, and his, and placed them back on the tray. He held out his arms and waited. Kate walked into them. As his arms circled her he pulled her close and kissed her long and hard. Kate put her arms around his neck and they swayed to the music.

"I don't know when I'll be back," said Declan against her hair.

"I know," Kate replied.

"You know I want you Kate,"

"I don't think…

"I could crash and burn on the runway tomorrow; then you'd be sorry." Kate tilted her head back, away from Declan, so she could look at him.

"I can't believe you used that old line on me. If you crash and burn on the runway, Declan Reynolds, I'll have your ashes put in a three minute egg timer on the mantelpiece, right there next to the clock…make you work for a change." Kate suddenly looked serious. "I can't bear for you to leave…not now." Declan kissed her. The only sound in the room was their breathing and that of the ticking clock. Still locked in a kiss, Declan lowered Kate to the couch.

The next morning Declan straightened his tie in the hallway mirror as he got ready to leave. "I've got to go Kate, I'll miss the train," he shouted up the stairs. Kate hurried down and threw herself into his arms as she came off the last step.

"Wait for me Kate. Don't go off and marry anyone," Declan said against her ear.

"I'll wait," she said. They kissed several times before Kate managed to close the door on him. She hurried to the bay window to watch him as he walked down the street.

Long letters, back and forth, kept the postman busy. Declan wrote that he'd flown several sorties. He didn't write about the planes that didn't come back or that his friend, Alec, had been shot down over France. Weeks turned into months but then Declan wrote that he had leave coming up and would be there around four o'clock the following Saturday.

Saturday afternoon Kate luxuriated in a hot bath. The claw-footed bath tub was large and deep. Kate lay in the water as a branch of the old lilac tree scratched at the window in a slight breeze. She closed her eyes and thought about the last time she and Declan made love. How many times she'd re-lived those moments in her dreams. Kate got out of the tub and wrapped herself in a towel. She stepped off the mat and onto the linoleum floor and padded down the hall to the bedroom. She decided to wear a soft green dress with short puff sleeves. She dabbed a little 'April in Paris' toilet water behind her ears and on the insides of her wrists. Downstairs she fussed with the cushions, wound the clock and frequently looked out the bay window to see if Declan was coming.

Declan walked quickly to Kate's house. He was dressed in uniform and had the ring in his pocket. He hadn't decided yet how he was going to ask Kate to marry him. Perhaps at the restaurant, tonight, before the meal was served, or he'd order champagne and then ask her.

When she heard the brass front door knocker being rapped, Kate ran to the door and flung it open to greet Declan. A man stood there in uniform. Kate didn't recognize him. The hat he wore low on his forehead. The name-tag above the wings on his jacket said 'McKenzie'. Kate's hand flew to her throat.

"Oh, my God, something's happened. Is he...has Declan been..."

"*No*," said the man placing his hand on her arm in reassurance. "I'm sorry...it's nothing like that." His accent was vaguely American.

"Then why are you here?"

"Kate, don't you know me? You look so much like Mum."

Kate, bewildered, stepped out into the street. "Harry? Oh, my God, Harry!" Kate hesitated for a moment then squealed and threw her arms around Harry's neck. She kissed his cheek, several times, and clung to him.

"I knew you'd come back, Harry...I just knew it. I've waited for...oh, Harry come in, come in." Kate pulled him into the house and closed the door. Declan stood on the corner of the street and watched. Anger rose up in him. How quickly love could turn to hate. He'd almost given her the ring and asked her to spend the rest of her life with him. What a bloody fool he'd been. Judging by the reception Kate gave the man; this had been going on for some time. He should go knock on her door and see what her reaction would be. She knew he was coming, how could she do this? Declan decided he'd catch the train and go back to the airfield. Or, maybe he'd get pissed as a newt at some pub on the way. He didn't know what he was going to do.

"Harry! I can't believe it's really you. Let me look at you. I want to hear everything." Harry looked around the room. Reading his thoughts Kate said, "She died of tuberculosis a long time ago. I didn't find out until I came back here."

"I didn't think she'd still be alive," said Harry. "She was so sick."

"Do you want to look round the house a bit while I get some glasses and something to drink. I've got some bottles of stout if that's alright?" Kate stopped in the doorway. "I still can't believe you're really here." Harry put his hat on the sideboard and walked around. His hand lingered on the newel post, at the bottom of the stairs, as he remembered his mother up in the front bedroom. He climbed the stairs as memories came flooding back. "I remember how hard you worked, Kate. You traded eggs for bread and milk. You used to boil Mum's sheets and our clothes in the copper and wrestle with that great monster of a mangle, in the back yard, to squeeze the water out."

"It's still out there and I still use it." Kate laughed.

"Everything looks so much smaller than I remember," Harry called out as he wandered around.

"You were a child then," said Kate from the kitchen. When Harry came back downstairs Kate placed a glass of the stout in his hand.

"Just like old times, you looking after me," said Harry.

"I want to know everything that happened after we were separated," said Kate. She sat down on the sofa, curled her legs under her and waited.

"I remember how terrified I felt getting taken away in the car. I'll never forget that feeling as long as I live. I was sent to a school, near London somewhere. I was treated well but remember feeling so...lost. I went on a ship to Canada and was taken in by the McKenzie's, in Toronto. They were a Scottish couple and owned a green-grocers shop. They were really good to me, Kate, and eventually adopted me. I think of them as my parents." Harry looked around the room as though the walls would hear the betrayal. "I went to school, grew up and met a girl. I joined up when the war started and was stationed over here."

"What made you come back to the house?" said Kate

"I came back as soon as I got to England. The house was empty. Don't know why I came today. I knocked on the door when I saw the curtains. Thought the owners wouldn't mind if I looked around. This place and you were part of my life. It always felt like something was missing. I never forgot you, Kate. Where did they send you?"

"Australia. I wasn't adopted like you, though. Louise Wilson, a nurse on the ship that took me to Australia, sort of took me under her wing. She became my guardian. I wanted to be just like her. I trained in Sydney then came back to England. I don't work too far from here. I had a good life in Australia, Harry."

"Then why did you come back?"

"I promised I'd take care of you and I couldn't. All I ever thought about was that someday you'd come back to this house. I had to know what happened to you. But we did alright, Harry. With our Dad not coming back from the war and then our mother gone, we'd have struggled and God only knows where we'd have ended up. Did you marry this girl?"

"Her name's Hannah. No, not yet, but she's the one." Kate put out her hand and touched Harry's face. "Mum and Dad would have been so proud of you, Harry."

"I'd like to think so. I think they'd have been proud of both of us, Kate. I know they'd have loved Hannah."

"I have someone special too. In fact you'll meet him tonight. He's someone I grew up with. He's in the R.A.F. so the two of you will have lots to talk about."

"What's his name?"

"Declan Reynolds. Don't know why he's so late. He should have been here ages ago." Kate got up, pulled the curtain aside and looked down the street."

"Will you stay…in this house?" asked Harry.

"No, it's yours now, Harry. You can come back here, with Hannah."

Harry shook his head. "There's nothing for me here but you, Kate. I'm a Canadian now. When the war's over I want to marry my girl and raise a family there."

The two talked long into the night…Kate listening for Declan's footsteps. After Harry was settled in the small bedroom, Kate came downstairs and worried about what could have happened to Declan? Trains were cancelled all the time because of tracks being bombed. Harry had made it here, though, but he'd come from a different direction. What if Declan had gone out on a sortie and not come back…what if he was…
Kate reached for the telephone as the clock on the mantelpiece chimed eleven.

Declan stretched out on the cot and put his hands behind his head. He'd come straight back on the train. The airman on the next cot snored loudly. Declan shouted to him to turn over, all the while seeing the picture, in his mind, of Kate throwing her arms around another man. How could she? He felt like such an idiot. He'd bared his soul to her because he trusted her. They grew up together. How could he have been so wrong about her? The anger festered and boiled in him. He got up and tipped the snoring man from his cot.

Kate called James. "You're right," he said. "It's not like him not to show up. I have the number of the squadron. Get a pencil and I'll give it to you."

"I'm so sorry to be calling so late James. I was just worried." James turned on the bedside lamp and looked at his watch on the table. "Don't worry yourself, Kate; I'm sure he's alright."

"What is it?" said Sadie, her head coming up off the pillow, her eyes still closed.

"Nothing…go back to sleep." Kate told James how Harry had come home, after all those years, just as she knew he would. She apologized again for bothering him. Kate dialed the number of the squadron and Declan was called to the phone.

"It's me, Kate. Are you alright? I was worried sick about you. I rang James…"

"Is that how you got this number?" Declan's voice snapped at her.

"I'm sorry. It was just…"

"I don't want to see you again. Got it?"

"*What*? What on earth are you talking about?"

"You know what I'm talking about. I saw you."

"Declan?" Kate's voice registered surprise.

"And don't call this number again. It's not for civilian use!" The 'phone disconnected and Kate was left listening to the dial tone before putting down the receiver. Declan had barely made it back to his cot when he was called to the 'phone a second time. "I told you…" he started.

"Declan, it's me, Uncle James. So, you're alright then? Kate called, she was worried about you."

"I'm fine! Kate already called."

"Good news about Harry, eh?"

"Harry?"

"Kate's brother. She always said he'd find his way back. Showed up tonight apparently."

"Harry, her brother?" said Declan his voice flat.

"Yes. Canadian Air Force…stationed here, didn't she tell you?"

"Uncle James, I've got to go. I have to call Kate." Declan tapped the phone and began dialing.

Suddenly the siren wailed and the pilots shot from their cots and ran from the Quonset huts throwing packs over their flight suits as they ran for the planes.

"Shit!" said Declan and slammed the 'phone down. The runway was full of activity, each man doing the job he'd been trained for. Propellers stuttered and revved into action. A loud drone of engines could be heard in the distance.

"Hurry, get those planes off the ground and out of here!" someone shouted above all the noise. Pilots, navigators, tail and turret gunners scrambled to put themselves into position for take-off. Each plane, Bombers and Spitfires taxied at random, circling the end of the runways. Searchlights snaked their way up into the sky giving a sense of urgency to every man on the field. The canopy of each Spitfire was slipped forward and closed during the taxi. The planes took off into the night…one after the other; Bombers heading one way, to a place of safety, while the Spitfires turned to intercept the enemy planes. The battle was intense. Each pilot, English and German played out his fate knowing that living was the only prize that mattered. Declan sat rigid in his seat, his teeth clenched and muscles taut as he fired a blaze of ammunition. Like looking through the lens of a camera, peripheral vision was reduced as Declan focused on the pilot and fuel tank of the enemy plane. A Spitfire spiraled down trailing black smoke as it headed towards the English coastline. Declan was too busy to wonder who it was. An enemy plane exploded in a burst of orange flame. Fragments of debris hurtled in every direction across the sky. Several pieces deflected off the canopy and nose of Declan's plane, some hitting the undercarriage on the way down. The Spitfires chased the retreating enemy planes out into the channel, away from the land.

"*Reynolds*!" The voice of the Squadron Commander crackled on the radio. "I see smoke… you're hit." Declan turned his head to look. "Roger," he said above the roar of the engine.

Each of the pilots, in what was left of the formation, came instantly alert to Reynolds emergency.

"I'm going low and dropping back," said Declan. The radio chattered as a plane came alongside. The pilot removed his goggles and mask. Declan waved at the familiar face.

Colin's voice filtered through the static on the radio. "I'll take a look," he said. Colin slipped behind the crippled plane to assess the damage. He pulled alongside again, shook his head and signaled a thumbs down. "It's a no go, Dec. Looks like a fuel leak," Colin's voice transmitted across the airwaves. "Could blow any time…bail-out." Declan nodded and began the procedure. The cockpit canopy refused to slide back.

"Bail out, *now* Declan. You don't have much time. I'm seeing flames, get out of there." The radio was still on.

"Shit! It's stuck. Canopy's jammed." Declan tugged harder to release it." Colin watched in horror. He knew every pilot's worse nightmare was being burned alive, trapped in his plane. The gun, the pilots carried, served a dual purpose. Declan pulled a knife out of a long pocket in his pants leg and tried to jimmy the canopy loose.

"It's no use it won't open. I'll get lower and see if I can put it down in the water."

"Negative," said Colin. "You'll break up in the water, fuel tank will blow or you'll be trapped and drown."

"Any other option?" said Declan, his voice calm and steady.

"Only one that I can think of… last resort though."

"Colin?"

"Yes, Dec.?"

"I did something stupid. I thought Kate was seeing another man. It was only her brother, Harry. Tell her I'm sorry and that ...tell her I love her." The radio went silent. "Did you hear me?" said Declan.

"I heard you," Colin replied.

CHAPTER NINETEEN
Waiting

John's hand hesitated a moment before he picked up the receiver. Louise came in from the porch. The screen smacked shut behind her as her husband picked up the 'phone.

"Still no news," said James. "I haven't called Kate yet...not until we know something definite. How are Louise and your mother taking it?"

"Like you'd expect."

"I'm sorry John. I should have some news by tonight. I'll ring you back."

"I'll stay near the 'phone. Thanks James." John put the receiver back down. Louise and Mum watched him expectantly. He shook his head. "Nothing yet." Louise went back outside and looked across the land seeing nothing, her bottom lip caught between her teeth. John followed her and put his arms around her. "I keep seeing him as a little boy," said Louise. "I can't bear the thought of him hurt or...or dead. I don't know where we're supposed to be right now. I want to go to England and find him but I'm afraid to be ten feet from the 'phone in case he calls. What'll we do? He's our son. I want him to come home." She turned to John her eyes full of tears.

"There's nothing we can do but wait, Louise. James is doing everything he can." John's voice sounded calm and consoling but the numbness he felt, after the first call, was gradually being replaced by anger. Every day, since Declan joined up, he and Louise jumped each time the phone rang. It was a call they'd always expected but, when it came, were unprepared for. John wanted the war over and his son home. Whichever way this went, with Declan, John had made up his mind to re-join the Anzacs.

Kate was changing the dressing on a young soldier's arm when a nurse came into the room. "I'll take over, Kate," she said. "You have a visitor in the office." Kate ran down the corridor knowing it had to be Declan but when she entered the room she saw Sadie.

"I had to come. It's Declan, he's…"

Kate backed away from her. "*No*," she said, her face crumpling into tears.

"It's not as bad as you think," said Sadie reaching her hand out to Kate.

Kate pushed Sadie's hand away as though touching would transfer the burden of truth.

"He's…missing. I wanted to come down and stay with you until we heard something. Now, get your things, love, and I'll take you home."

"Does Louise and…"

"Yes. James telephoned them. James wasn't going to tell you, until he knew something definite, but I thought it best you were told."

"Declan was angry with me. I don't know why. He said he didn't want to see me again. Those were the last words he said to me. I love him Sadie. What am I going to do without him?"

"Now don't be jumping to conclusions. We'll just have to wait and see." At home Kate sat in the fireside chair while Sadie stretched out on the couch. The clock chimed five a.m. "I can't just sit here," said Kate. "I'll go mad."

"Then why don't you go up to bed and have a lie down. I'll listen for the 'phone."

"Sadie's right," said Harry, who stood at the window.

"No. I need to be at work, keep myself busy. I'm going back to the hospital." Sadie got up as Kate went to the hallway and took her coat off the newel post.

"You can't go out in the dark," said Harry.

"I don't want to be here when the 'phone rings," said Kate. With that she left, closing the front door behind her.

Harry said, "I'll go with her."

"No," said Sadie. "Let her go."

As Kate walked down the street the tears came. From the ward, Kate looked out of the window that overlooked the street outside the hospital. It was that time of the morning when the darkness starts to lighten, just before the sun rises. The ward was silent. No-one was awake yet. Kate heard shoes squeaking across polished linoleum.

"I'm replacing you," said the young nurse. "There's someone to see you in the office." Kate nodded and walked across the ward and down the corridor. She hesitated and took a deep breath before opening the door. A uniformed man stood next to the desk.

"*Declan*," Kate cried out. Declan strode across the room and the two embraced. "Forgive me Kate. I thought you were seeing someone else. I didn't know it was Harry."

"It doesn't matter," said Kate. "You're here and you're alive. I don't care about anything else." Her eyes were bright with tears. Declan pulled away and took something out of his pocket. It was a small black velvet box; one that had traveled from England to Australia and back again.

"I was going to give it to you, that last night." He opened the box, took out the ring and slipped it onto her finger.

Back in Willoughby John's mother and Louise stood side by side clutching hands.

"Yes, Yes, I can hear you," said John.

Louise saw John's expression of relief and heard the excitement in his voice. He put the 'phone against his chest. "He's alright. He's back in England. His canopy jammed. He managed to get it open, last minute. A fishing boat on the French side picked him up." He spoke into the receiver again. "Yes, it is good news, James."

Louise and Mum hugged each other. John raised his hand for silence. "What? What did you say, James?" John put the 'phone to his chest again then put it back to his ear. "You sure?"

"Positive," said James.

"What is it? Tell me before I burst all over this kitchen," said Louise.

"Declan. He gave her a ring…they're engaged."

"He's *what*? Who?" said Louise.

"Kate." John grinned and said back into the 'phone, "second best news I've heard all day. You too James. Thanks for everything. John put down the 'phone.

"Well I'll be…" he said.

"'bout time," said Mum. Louise and John looked at the old woman. "He wrote and told me he was thinking about asking her. A blind man could see those two were perfect for each other. Why'd you think I gave him the ring?"

"There's something else," said John. "I'm going back into the Army." Louise sat down abruptly on the kitchen chair.

"You're too old," said Mum.

"Apparently not. I won't be in the thick of it but I can be of some use. I want this war over and done with before I do lose my son. Stand beside me on this one Louise. I need you to tell me you're alright with this."

"Well," said Mum. "This is for the two of you to sort out. I've got knitting to do. That grandson of mine is probably going to make a great-grandma out of me and I'm suddenly feeling quite old." John waited for Mum to leave. "What do you say, Louise?"

"No! It's not enough that I have to worry myself sick about Declan and Kate but now you want to put me through worrying about you too. I won't do it. You're needed *here*, John. You had your turn in the last war and they can't ask more of you. Truth be told, you've never gotten over it. I hear you at night, sometimes. On the rare occasions you *do* talk to me about the war it was as though it happened yesterday. Why would you want to go back to that? You have two daughters who need a father. What if you don't come back...how am I supposed to go on?" Louise was shouting, her voice high pitched in anger.

"I can understand how you feel..." John started but Louise cut him off.

"You can't possibly understand how I feel. You're too selfish. I lost a husband, nearly lost someone I think of as my son and now you want to..." Louise got up and walked out the back door. She slammed the screen deliberately. Arms folded she strode out past the Gum tree.

Henry stood up. "Are you alright, Missus?"

"No, I'm bloody well not!"

"Is it Mr. Declan?"

Her voice softened. "No, he's alright. Mr. Mannington just called. Declan's fine."

"But you are upset."

"That...that man wants me to say it's alright for him to go back in the Army." She pointed to the house. "Not enough we nearly lost Declan... now *he* wants to go too." Louise paced back and forth, hands on her hips.

Henry looked thoughtful for a moment. "But maybe...that's where Mr. Reynolds is supposed to be, Missus. He is a father. When someone tries to kill a man's son he has a duty to protect his family. It is his *need* to go... not his want." Henry's voice was soft, each word slow and precise.

"This is why he must go and you must let him, Missus."

Louise stopped pacing, surprised at the depth of the old man's understanding. In her heart Louise knew that what Henry was saying was true.

"But it isn't fair." She sounded like a child as she stuffed her hands deep in her apron pockets.

"War is never...fair," said Henry.

"Do *you* have family, somewhere, Henry? Were you ever married?"

"No." Henry shook his head. "Too much worry."

Louise managed a smile and expelled a breath along with her anger.

"You're a very wise man, Henry."

"That is what I tell the foreman...all the time." Henry grinned displaying the missing teeth.

"What made you stay here, Henry? We used to worry you'd go on a walkabout and never come back?"

"I am African, not Aborigines. I don't go on walkabout."

"How did you get here?"

"On a ship. I went to a missionary school in Africa, learned to speak English... very well. When I was old enough I signed on with a ship. I liked the sea but when I got older I became tired of it. I wanted land under my feet."

"Why here?"

"I like *here*. This is my home. I will die in this place." Louise studied the old man for a moment. She reached out and patted his arm and said, "Thank you."

"For what, Missus?"

"The advice, and for listening. I'll see you in the morning."

"Goodnight, Missus."

"'Night Henry." John was still sitting at the kitchen table when Louise came in.

"What would you say if I asked you not to go?" said Louise.

"I'd still go but I'd rather you were on my side."

Louise stood behind him and placed her hands on his shoulders and gently squeezed. "When do you have to leave?"

"In three days."

"I'll help you pack your things."

"Then you're alright with me going?"

"Not really but I know that it's something you feel you have to do…so I'm with you."

"John took a deep breath. "You're not mad anymore?"

"I was, but not now. You're a good man and I love you. I hope I tell you that often enough. Just come back to me."

"What made you change your mind?"

"Henry."

Louise folded a couple of shirts, a pair of trousers, underwear and rolled socks before putting them in John's suitcase. He wouldn't need much as he'd be in uniform most of the time. She remembered the last time when she'd packed David's things before he went off to war in France. She'd felt a pang of sadness and abandonment at his leaving. She'd tucked a note between David's shirts for him to find, telling him how much she loved him. She never saw him again. Mum stood in the bedroom doorway. "He'll be alright. He's got his wits about him that one." She patted Louise's hand.

"I hope you're right."

Louise kept herself busy helping doctor Phillips in his surgery. She planted a kitchen garden with carrots, potatoes, radishes and lettuce, putting netting over the top to keep the rabbits out but, they got in anyway. She cried over the loss but, it wasn't the garden she was so upset about. She wanted everyone home and safe. For most of her life she'd worried about somebody.

CHAPTER TWENTY
Destruction

Sadie came into the study. In her hands she held two very large whiskeys. She handed one to James.

"What's this in aid of?" he asked.

"Nothing," said Sadie. Sadie put her glass on the table and sat across James's lap. She put her arms around his neck. "You want something," said James, his look wary.

"No, came to tell you something. I thought it would be nice to have a dinner party, just Declan and Kate…sort of an engagement celebration. Nothing fancy." To an observer the two were just an older couple, but neither James nor Sadie saw that in each other.

"When," asked James.

"Tonight. Declan and Kate should be on the train already." Sadie looked at her watch.

"What have you planned for dinner? said James.

"Cod, chips and mushy peas, followed by treacle pudding and I'm serving it on the good silver. Thomas said I should."

"James rolled his eyes upward. "Don't ever change Sadie."

"So, you're not sorry you married me?"

"Never." James kissed her.

Sadie smiled at him and climbed off his lap.

"I'll send Thomas in to help you change, shall I?" Sadie didn't wait for a reply. James wheeled himself a little closer to the fire and watched it light up the whiskey in his glass to a rich deep amber. He sighed with contentment.

Meanwhile, Declan and Kate rushed for the train. The steam hissed and belched out from under the wheels. They jumped aboard and found a vacant compartment with upholstered seats facing each other. Oval mirrors were screwed to the wall above each seat. Declan threw the suitcases on the rack overhead. A whistle sounded and the train shunted out of the station and was soon in the countryside. Fields of sheep and villages of thatched cottages flashed by as the train gathered speed.

"Don't you wonder what the people, who live in those houses, are like?" said Kate. "I imagine them happy, the house cozy, and the wife listening to the wireless while she gets tea ready for the children."

"Have you thought about where *you* want to live, after we're married?" said Declan.

"Willoughby," replied Kate without hesitation. "I want to live in Willoughby."

"What about your parent's house, will Harry live there?"

"No. He'll go back to Canada after the war. We decided we'd sell it."

The train began to stop. It screeched as the friction of metal wheels clenched against the track. Declan and Kate were thrown from their seats. A suitcase fell down from the overhead net as the train came to a sudden halt.

"You alright?" said Declan helping Kate to her feet.

"Yes, I think so."

"I'll go and see what's happened."

The clacking of the train had masked the roar of the plane and the sound of bullets strafing the front engine. Declan looked out of the window and saw the plane with its black cross insignia.

"One of ours?" asked Kate, unable to see, when she heard the engine.

"No. He'll turn and come back," said Declan throwing open the carriage door.

"We've got to get under the train." Declan grabbed Kate's arm, dragged her through the open door and pushed her under the train. Doors were beginning to open and people stood for a moment looking confused. "Get under the train!" Declan shouted at them.

Kate lay flat on her stomach between the tracks. She could smell hot oil on metal and was oblivious to the gravel scraping her knees. Kate put her hands over her ears when she heard the plane coming back and looked around for Declan. Some of the passengers were soldiers. They barked out orders to the civilians and picked positions to fire at the lone German plane. People screamed in panic. The German pilot came in low over the hedges, lining up for strafing. The pilot was an easy target for a well-placed shot by one of the soldiers. The plane careened over the top of the train and into a field. Its left wing clipped a raised furrow and cart-wheeled, breaking apart as it made contact with the ground. Declan talked to a group of soldiers as the people crawled out from under the train.

"What do you think he was doing out here alone?"

"He wasn't alone, look." The soldier pointed off in the distance. Two bombers were being escorted by a squadron of German planes.

"How in the hell did they get this far inland?" said Declan.

"Won't get much further," said the soldier. "Here comes the welcoming committee." The noise was deafening as the horizon became dotted with Spitfires…too many to count. The people from the train cheered and clapped their hands as the aerial battle began. The German bombers veered away.

Back at Baden Hall Sadie was setting the table and fiddling with the flowers in the centre vase. She'd filled it with pink Peonies, cream Roses and blue Delphiniums from the garden greenhouse.

Thomas was helping James get dressed in the bedroom, off the study. Sadie hummed to herself, she didn't even know the name of the tune… something she'd heard on the wireless. She stopped humming for a moment and froze in place when she heard the whistle of the bombs.

"*James!*" she screamed and ran for the bedroom.

The explosion knocked her backwards, off her feet. The lead-paned windows and masonry, having stayed intact for centuries, collapsed into the room. Sadie lay in the rubble for some time. She awoke disoriented. Masonry dust enveloped everything. Sadie coughed and moved her arms and legs, then pushed herself up onto her hands and knees. Pictures had fallen, still attached to pieces of wall. The table was buried under debris. Sadie looked up, her face and hair coated with white powdered stone. She could see the sky. Her ears were ringing and she felt dizzy. Her eyes burned. She moved slowly to get herself upright picking her way carefully over the rubble.

"*James!*" Sadie called to him, repeatedly, as she made her way towards the bedroom.

As she turned the corner she saw only the outdoors. She could see all the way to the lake. The bedroom was no longer there. Half the house was gone. Sadie made no sound but sank to her knees, her mind unable to accept the scene spread out before her. That's where the villagers found her, on her knees with a look of absolute horror on her face. The twisted remains of James's chair had blown a long way from the house.

CHAPTER TWENTY-ONE
A Visitor

Declan sat in the Quonset hut writing a letter to Gran. He didn't tell her about how fearful he'd become about every mission these days. He took less risk, kept firing his guns even when he knew his opponent was finished. He didn't want to be the one to lose his life. When he'd first joined up he was eager, full of confidence and ego. He'd felt invincible. It was a game played out in the sky. Something he and the other flyers bragged about over a pint at the local pub. As the war dragged on every sortie he flew he wondered if this was it. It was a game of Russian Roulette. He tended to look at everything as though he were seeing it for the first and last time. There was no more boasting and no laughter among the squadron, in fact they barely talked to each other.

Tempers frayed from intense tiredness. The gravity of their situation kept morale low. Every moment with Kate was filled with passion, both anticipating it might be the last time. Everything had more meaning. Minutes were precious. He wanted to live and wanted to dream of a future with Kate. Instead he wrote that his friend, Colin, had married a village girl. Many of the airmen had married wanting someone and something to come back to. A sense of home and family. Declan asked Gran how Sadie was doing, since her return. He told her the bombs had come from the two German bombers. Since they couldn't reach their target they released the bombs on everything in their path before they were shot down. He asked about Henry and about Willoughby. A little economical with the truth, he told her he'd be home soon. Fact of it was he didn't know when he'd be home or if he ever would. Declan listened to the rain beat against the metal roof. Loud as it was it was somehow soothing. At the end of the room several airmen surrounded a trestle table. They played cards, as a diversion, until the next orders came. The door opened and Colin came rushing in.

"Officer…high rank too."

"Where?" said Declan.

"Right behind me." Chairs scraped back, on the concrete floor, as every man stood to attention.

"At ease," said the visitor.

"*Surprise*," said Colin. Declan, whose eyes had been fixed straight ahead, turned to look at the figure the voice belonged to. He narrowed his eyes. "Dad? What in the world are you doing here…and in that uniform?"

The two men embraced and thumped each other on the back. The card game resumed.

"Went back in. Once an Anzac always an Anzac."

"No-one said anything to me."

"Told them not to."

"What are you doing in England?"

"There's a big push to get this war finished up, thought you could use a hand." John removed his gloves, topcoat and hat.

"Is that true? *We* haven't heard anything," said Colin.

"It's no secret," said John.

"How long have you been here in England and where are you staying?"

Declan was animated as he fired one question after the next. "I've got a meeting in London tomorrow morning. Any place we can get food here, I'm starving?" said John. "I have a car and a driver, we could go somewhere."

"Rank does have its privileges. Got to go," said Colin. He pulled up his collar and headed out into the rain.

"I can't leave," said Declan. He strode to the door and stuck his head out.

"Colin, see if you can scrounge something to eat will you?" Declan looked at his father. "There's fog rolling in. Don't think we'll get called out tonight but you never know."

"A reprieve." said John."

"Something like that." John looked at his son.

He saw the tiredness etched in his face, the darkness under his eyes. "How did you do it, Dad? Get through all this. It's what you were trying to tell me when I joined up, wasn't it? I feel so…so old."

John thought for a moment. "Yes, I know the feeling. The last war took part of me with it. My youth was left behind on the battlefields. You get through it, Declan, the best you can. When it's all over you'll never take anything for granted again. You'll realize that family is all that's important. You'll make a good life for yourself with Kate and that's what you hold on to. It's your reason to come back. I can't divulge what I know but trust me, this war is going to be over very soon, I promise you. Just hang on a little longer."

Declan smiled as a shout came from the end of the room. Someone had won the pot and there were groans from the losers.

"How's everything back home and how's Sadie doing?" said Declan.

"Everyone's fine. Sadie's starting to function again. I think she'll be alright."

"Why did you go back into the Army, Dad?"

"I want this war over so my son can come h…" A siren began to rev up to a full wail before John could finish his sentence. Father and son looked each other in the eyes.

"I've got to go, Dad," said Declan. The two hugged each other, reluctant to let go.

"Look after Kate if I don't…" John nodded and watched as Declan ran in the pouring rain for his plane. John watched as the plane taxied out. Declan waved and then was gone.

CHAPTER TWENTY-TWO
Full Circle

Church bells rang all over the city. They were ringing in every town and village all over Britain. The sound pealed out the message of victory and an end to the war. The word victory was interpreted by weary Britons as freedom, peace and homecoming…not winning. Not immediately.

Kate ran down the ward and put her head out the window. The patients looked alarmed. "What is it?" said Kate shouting to anyone who would listen.

A woman in a paisley headscarf, knotted under her chin, shouted up. "War's over. It was on the wireless." Some of the invalids got out of bed, some couldn't.

"Did I hear right, the war's over?" said one man.

"Yes," said Kate.

"Bloody 'ell," said the man.

Kate and the nurses whooped with joy and ran through the wards with the news. People spilled into the streets cheering, dancing and hugging each other in a display of happiness not seen in years and rarely demonstrated in public. All night the people hung about in the streets.

After her shift, Kate made her way to the house. Never had she seen people so happy. Their loved ones were coming home, they had reason to celebrate. For so many, peace had come too late to bring home a husband, a father, a son. Buried where they died, on foreign soil, they'd never be coming home. A photograph on a mantelpiece all that was left to show they ever existed. Over the years the women had clamored around posted lists of the dead and wounded. It was like a lottery to see who had won and who had lost. It was all over now, thought Kate. She was so proud of the women who filled the men's places in the munitions factories, lived on tripe, rabbit, pigeons, sheep's brains and cabbage and never complained.

They donated saucepans, anything metal, even their wedding rings to be melted down for the war effort. It was all over…at last. If Declan and John were still alive it wouldn't be long before she heard. Kate refused to look at the lists like the other women.

Back in Willoughby Louise and Mum stood back and looked. "That's the most pathetic looking Christmas tree I've ever set eyes on," said Sadie.

"Well, it'll be alright if it's done up a bit," said Mum.

"It's not straight, looks crooked to me," said Sadie.

"Where did you get it?" asked Mum.

"Look, old woman, it's the best I could do. It's a tree…grant you it's not a Christmas tree but it'll have to do," said Sadie trying to straighten out the tree.

Louise laughed. "Nothing ever changes with you two does it?" Louise unpacked a box of Christmas tree ornaments that were wrapped in tissue paper. Every Christmas she gave all the girls an ornament so that when they grew up, married and left home they'd have ornaments for their own tree. It wouldn't be long before that happened.

"Alice," said Mum. "You and Margaret can get started on the tree if you like, There's tinsel in the box. Us old folks are going outside to put our feet up for a minute."

Alice was tall like her father but had Maggie's looks. She had no aspirations to go to college. She liked things of a domestic nature. She wanted to be a wife, mother and loved to cook and sew. She was a bit of a tomboy in some ways and could ride a horse as well as Declan. She could sheer sheep and deliver lambs with the best of the hands. Alice had her eye on a young man, the son of a local farmer.

Margaret had always known what she wanted to do with her life. There was a need for a good veterinarian in Willoughby. She looked a little like Louise but there was much about her like her grandmother. She was direct and straightforward.

"Got some nice bottles of cider Sadie brought me from England," said Mum. "Says Scrumpy on the label. Thought we could sit on the porch and have a glass."

"Best idea you've had all day," said Sadie.

The three women stretched out in the chairs and said nothing for a few moments. They sipped the strong crisp cider and felt the cares of the day slip away.

"I can't wait for John and the children to get back tomorrow," said Louise.

"They made it through. I can't believe it's all over," said Sadie.

"It'll be nice to get back to some normalcy," said Louise. Mum dredged the last of the cider from her glass, smacked her lips and went back into the house for a refill.

"Too many of those and you won't live to be a good old girl," yelled Sadie.

"Mind your business," Mum retorted.

Sadie laughed. "She's a character that one. Wouldn't have her any different though."

"She's a good woman," said Louise. A silence fell between the two women.

"I'm going back to England, Louise. I'm going to rebuild the Hall and open it up as an hotel. I've already talked to Declan about it. He doesn't want to live there. After I'm gone it'll be his…for his children."

"I'm not sure it's a good idea to go back so soon," said Louise.

"I spent the happiest years of my life there. I've got to keep busy, Louise. I'll be back and forth between there and Willoughby. I won't be gone for good."

"I'm truly sorry about James," Louise said.

Sadie laughed with sarcasm. "Wasn't even enough to bury but, I put what was left of his chair in the ground and there's a headstone."

"Ironic isn't it," said Sadie. "To lose two men, I loved, to war. I don't know where my fiancé was buried and there's nothing left of James. I suppose I wasn't meant to be with anyone."

"You were loved twice in your life, like me. That's something to hold on to." Mum elbowed her way through the screen door and plunked herself back in her chair.

"They're going to think we're daft having Christmas in February. Never heard of such a thing," said Sadie. The old woman looked serious. "It'll be good to have everyone back where they belong," she said.

"Sadie's going back to England, Mum," said Louise. "She's going to make Baden Hall into an hotel."

"Ay, I heard. Might be going back that way, meself." Louise and Sadie looked surprised and stopped rocking.

"Whatever for?' said Sadie.

"I'm getting on, not got many more good years left. I want to see Yorkshire one last time. I want to bring my little girl back and bury her here".

"You had a daughter?" said Sadie. "I thought John was an only child?"

"John said he had a sister…that she'd died when she was little," said Louise. Mum took another sip of the cider. "Dad and I …we didn't talk about it. She was a bonnie little thing. I can see her clear as day and I still remember her laugh."

"What happened?" said Louise.

"Emma, that was her name, got sick. Diphtheria they said. Nothing anyone could do. It was my punishment." Mum took another sip of the cider.

"Punishment for what?" said Sadie.

"She wasn't Dad's. She was his brother's child." Louise and Sadie were stunned into silence for a moment.

"Did Dad know?" said Sadie.

"Yes, he knew. I'd never been with Dad before I married him. I was friends with him but I loved his brother, Alphonse. Al couldn't stay in one place for very long. He was wild and exciting. Brothers yes, but they were nothing alike."

"Why are you telling us this now," said Louise.

"I'm getting old, love. Maybe it's the cider or it's just good to tell somebody…I don't know,"

"So what happened?" asked Sadie.

"Al denied it was his child, said it was Dad's. I was never with anyone else but Al. He was angry and left. It would have been such a scandal, in my day, and living where everyone knew everyone else, you know how it is. I didn't know what I was going to do. Dad said he'd loved me all along but I hadn't noticed, too wrapped up with Al. I was young. Dad was solid, dependable and he was good to me. He married me to spare me the shame. He and his brother never spoke again but I heard from Al over the years. He said he was sorry and sent me a ticket to join him here, in Willoughby, but I told him it was too late. He built this house for me thinking I'd come but, by then, I was in love with Dad. Funny how things work out isn't it?" Louise got up and squatted in front of the old woman. She put her hands around both of hers. "I can't let you go all that way by yourself. What do you say you and I go with Sadie to England? I'll go with you up to Yorkshire and we'll bring your little girl home."

"I'll go too. I've never been to Yorkshire," said Sadie.

"That's all I want," said Mum, her chin trembling.

Sadie cleared her throat of emotion. "Where did you hide the cider? I think I could use another drop." Louise got up and went into the house returning with two bottles. "I think if we're going to get drunk we'd better make a good job of it," she said.

Next morning the budgerigars twittered in the trees as soon as the sun came up. The house was a beehive of activity as last minute housework was taken care of. Sleeves were turned up to the elbows as the women set about rolling out pastry to make apple pies. A joint of beef was put in the oven to roast and Mum dropped an egg into a well of flour to make Yorkshire pudding. Potatoes were pared and carrots simmered in a steaming pot that clattered its lid for attention.

"They're here, I see the car," shouted Alice shading her eyes as she stood on the porch. Louise took off her apron and walked quickly outside. Her pace increased when she saw the car in the distance, until she was running. She kept running past the fence and out to the road and continued to run until the car stopped in a cloud of dust. The driver's door flew open and Louise was in John's arms.

That evening John went outside to smoke a cigarette. He walked past the Gum tree. Henry stood up.

"What are you doing out here, Henry? You have a comfortable bed in the bunkhouse."

The old man laughed. "I sleep in it too. My bones are getting too old to be sleeping on the ground. I come out here to reflect on things. This tree and me are old friends." Henry patted his hand on the trunk.

John looked up at the branches. "It's been here as long as I can remember," he said.

"It is silent witness to our lives, Mr. Reynolds."

"I suppose you're right, Henry." John looked towards the house. In the darkness, yellow light shone from every window of the large rambling house. John thought about the first time he'd come here to Willoughby, thought about the cold morning he'd crawled out to save James Mannington and the twists and turns his life had taken since then. There were times he'd wished he hadn't saved James but then he wouldn't have

Declan. John wondered what would have happened if he'd driven Maggie to town that day. Over the years he'd forgiven himself for not doing so. He would always remember and love Maggie. Alice was a constant reminder of her. He loved Louise equally. Coming home always made him appreciate what a good life he had here. The house looked like a jewel in the night. It wasn't Baden Hall with its elegance and servants. No need to dress up for dinner. It was a real 'put your feet up' kind of home…a place to come back to and shuck off the worries of the world. John tossed his cigarette and ground it into the dirt.

"I'll see you in the morning, Henry, goodnight."

"Goodnight Mr. Reynolds." John stepped up onto the porch. He heard laughter and stopped to look through the window into the kitchen. The glass was wavy and distorted, made on site when the house was built. He wished his father were here now. How much he missed him. He imagined the sweet smell of Dad's tobacco and remembered him on the porch waxing the cradle for his first grandchild.

"Hope for a son." His father's voice echoed in his memory. "Someone to pass this on to. We've worked so hard, it'd be a shame to lose it." And Maggie, forever young in his memory…ghosts that crept between his mind and his heart.

John stood in the darkness and peered through the window at his son, his daughters, Mum, Sadie and Kate. He felt contentment unlike anything he'd ever felt before. It was like opening a box and seeing everything you've ever wanted inside.

END

FOOTNOTE

The research for this story of fiction took several years. I was privileged to visit Australia. An ad in an Australian newspaper resulted in a letter from an elderly woman who described the voyage. She had not added her name or return address but her descriptions of her journey, aboard ship, moved me to tears.

Should you wish to know the true story about these migrant children please go to: Wikipedia: Home Children. Book: 'Empty Cradles' by Margaret Humphry's, the courageous woman who exposed this tragedy. DVD: 'Oranges and Sunshine', the story of Margaret Humphrey's. Great Britain did apologize to the migrants in 2010.

ABOUT THE AUTHOR

A.E. Connors was born and educated in England. She was raised in Leicester, in the Midlands of the U.K. At present she resides in Colorado.

WILLOUGHBY, The story of an Empire's shame, was inspired by her mother who was one of the few migrant children to make her way home to England.

Please feel free to contact the author via e-mail at lizmark1@aol.com